A THEOLOGY OF MARRIAGE

CONTEMPORARY COLLEGE THEOLOGY SERIES

GENERAL EDITORS: J. FRANK DEVINE, S.J.
BOSTON COLLEGE

RICHARD W. ROUSSEAU, S.J.
FAIRFIELD UNIVERSITY

A THEOLOGY OF MARRIAGE is one of the volumes in the Christian Living section of this series.

A
Theology of Marriage

A doctrinal, moral, and legal study

CHARLES P. KINDREGAN

Assistant Professor, Loyola University of Chicago

THE BRUCE PUBLISHING COMPANY / Milwaukee

NIHIL OBSTAT:

JOHN A. SCHULIEN, S.T.D.
Censor librorum

IMPRIMATUR:

✛ WILLIAM E. COUSINS
Archbishop of Milwaukee
July 10, 1967

The *Nihil obstat* and *Imprimatur* are a declaration that a book or pamphlet is considered to be free from doctrinal or moral error. It is not implied that those who have granted the *Nihil obstat* and *Imprimatur* agree with the contents, opinions, or statements expressed.

TO TRISH

Library of Congress Catalog Card Number: 67–26508

EDITORS' INTRODUCTION

THE CONTEMPORARY COLLEGE THEOLOGY SERIES

This series begins with the presupposition that theology is necessary. It is necessary if Christian intelligence is to search for meaning in its dialogue with God, man, and the world. Since Christian intelligence is not the exclusive possession of the theological specialist or the cleric, the search must be carried on in all those areas of life, secular as well as religious, including the college situation, where meaning is to be found.

This search is a peaceful one, for in some mysterious way it has already achieved its goal: the vision of faith and the fullness of love. Still it remains a relentless and universal search. Its inner certainty must radiate out not only to the edges of the mind but also into the farthest recesses of the world. We could call it "lay" theology, but this word seems too pale a description for such an exciting enterprise of the Christian life.

In view of this, the editors of this series are convinced that new questions had to be asked, new structures created, and new books written. These books would be neither catechetical nor apologetic. They would be purely and simply theological. The primary audience would be believers, but all thinking men would find them useful. In scope they would be broad enough to ensure perspective. They would be scholarly enough to be intellectually relevant. They would avoid pedantry. In short, they would try to present a rich and deep understanding of Christian revelation in such a way that today's college students would be able to respond with a Christian faith and life that are both culturally mature and scientifically precise. Finally, the authors of these books would be, for the most part, teachers in colleges and universities where much of the contemporary theological dialogue is now going on.

The series falls into four parts: biblical, historical, ecclesial, and ethical. The divisions were not predetermined by the editors. They follow the shape of the most vigorous theological work now being done.

The books in the biblical section are intended to go beyond the traditional treatment of Bible history and the now familiar perspectives of salvation history. They concentrate on various books of the Bible. Their method has been especially designed for college work. Tentatively it might be called "exegetical theology." Every verse is not considered after the fashion of a commentary, nor are narratives developed as a biography, nor is there any attempt to create large theological syntheses. Rather the individual books are studied in chronological sequence; key passages are treated in detail and the rest are summarized. At the same time some attention is paid to the growing theological synthesis.

Since scholastic theology is already represented by individual works and sets of textbooks, the books in our historical section study dogmatic questions from a developmental point of view. In this way the editors hope to make the college students more aware of the great wealth of theological thinking that recent historico-theological studies have uncovered. This method which is more inductive than deductive should happily coincide with the thought processes of the college student. The three basic poles for synthesis are: God, Christ, and Man. In each area the historical development will be studied and a significant number of basic source texts presented. The problems raised in these studies will range all the way from Augustinian pessimism to Teilhardian optimism.

The textbooks for the third part of the series will deal with issues of great contemporary importance. They will examine questions discussed by the Second Vatican Council. As the name implies, ecclesial theology must first concern itself with the Church, what the Church knows herself to be, as expressed in the insights of the new Constitution on the Church and with the more significant of the Church's allied concerns: other world religions, American Protestantism, its history, its motivating forces and spirit, and finally the new sacramental theology so enriched by the many magnificent liturgical advances. All of this growth has brought a wider and deeper appreciation of the nature of the Roman Catholic Church and her relationship rooted in understanding and love with the whole world.

The fourth and final section of the series is devoted explicitly to Christian moral response. The editors subscribe to the position that the proper place for the Catholic college or university to examine ethical questions is in a revelational rather than in a purely philosophical context. In addition to the "virtue" divisions of the Summa or the classic moral theology text, designed primarily for confessors, there is a need and a place for a "Christian ethics" that reflects the new insight which both biblical and dogmatic theology can provide. These books will strive to be openly Christian in spirit, eclectic in approach, up to date in scholarship, and will address themselves to those ethical problems which are most real to the modern American mind.

Finally, the editors would like to express their thanks to all those whose interest, advice, and cooperation have made this series possible. They are especially grateful to Mr. William May of The Bruce Publishing Company, who not only initiated the project and sustained it through the inevitable disappointments and complications, but contributed so much of his editorial skill to its final shape. To the individual authors who so graciously added to their heavy burden of academic responsibility by undertaking these books, we can only express the hope that their share in the shaping and influencing of the American Catholic community of today and of tomorrow will be far more meaningful to them than any meager thanks of ours.

> The Editors,
> REV. J. FRANK DEVINE, S.J., Boston College
> REV. RICHARD W. ROUSSEAU, S.J., Fairfield University

AUTHOR'S
INTRODUCTION

This volume centers on the theme of a man and woman achieving holiness in a communion of one flesh. The phrase "one flesh," expresses the fundamental Judeo-Christian conception of marital love. It is used in the text of Gen 2:24 to define the essence of marriage; Jesus bases his teaching about marriage on it in Mt 19:5; for the apostle Paul, the one flesh is a great mystery which partakes of the unity of Christ and the Church, Eph 5:31-32. One flesh is perhaps a weak expression of the scriptural proclamation. For the man of biblical faith a union of flesh was a total union of two human beings who thereby created a vital, new being. A new human person, consequently, is created by marriage — a person both sanctified and sanctifying in the mysteries of creation and redemption.

Specific Subject Matter

Determining the subjects to be treated in a text of this kind presents real difficulties. A survey of college catalogues and a number of professors teaching the course convinced the author that the content is diversified from school to school. A brief word on the factors bearing on the final choice of subject matter is therefore in order. The primary determinant of content is the author's experience in evolving his own course over a period of years. The advice of other professors who are active in this area was also quite important. Contemporary interest was a factor; it explains, for example, the length of the chapters on the procreation of children and the limitation of births. The influence of the Second Vatican Council affected not only what is written but the subjects discussed; a good example is the extensive treatment of sex education which was included because of the requests by the Council that Catholic schools and parents begin to take this phase of Christian education seriously. Hundreds of student comments collected by the author provided still another guide in the choice of subjects. Inclusion of material on the engagement and budgeting are examples. Traditional course content had its influence; it is hard to imagine a college course in marriage which does not provide some information on the law of marriage, for example. Certain subjects, such as dating and widowhood, were minimized or excluded, not because they are unimportant but because they appear to be rarely discussed.

Sources

There are two principal sources used in this volume, both of which should be quite familiar to college students of theology. These are the Scriptures and the documents issued by the Second Vatican Council. The *Revised Standard Version of the Holy Bible*, the modern descendant of the great King James Version, is quoted throughout the text. *The Documents of Vatican II*, edited by Walter Abbott and Joseph Gallagher, provides the translations of Conciliar texts used in this volume. Other sources used are the writings of the Fathers of the Church; these translations are based on the classic Migne's *Patrologiae Cursus Completus*, published in Paris between 1844 and 1886. Historic, formal statements on Christian doctrine by Popes or Councils are translated from *Denzinger Enchiridion Symbolorum*, edited by Adolfus Schönmetzer (1963); this is cited in the footnotes as *Denz*. Recent papal teachings are from the *Acta Apostolicae Sedis*; this is cited as A.A.S. (*Acta Sanctae Sedis*, A.S.S., before 1909).

Personal Acknowledgments

I am indebted to many persons; to my wife Patricia, I am indebted beyond calculation. Without her this book would not have been written nor my life be as full as it is.

Charles P. Kindregan

March 8, 1967
Loyola University of Chicago

CONTENTS

PART IV THE HUMAN LAW OF MARRIAGE

TOWARD A THEOLOGY OF MARRIAGE

CHAPTER 1

THE NEED FOR A THEOLOGY
OF MARRIAGE

Most adult Christians are married. They recognize that certain actions should be avoided in their marital life because of their Christian faith. They can define marriage as a sacrament by which they receive grace to carry out the duties of their state in life. Yet few, married Catholics possess a vision of their marriage as the very substance of their Christian experience. They might dissent from John Calvin's view that marriage is no more of a religious act than is farming a field, building a house, or mending a shoe,[1] but few, married Christians could explain how the taking of a wife or husband is related to their participation in the mysteries of creation and redemption. Is this situation desirable? After all, it is apparent that only a few Christians can be theologians. There are some who would no doubt argue that it is sufficient for the majority of

---

[1] *The Institutes of the Christian Religion*, Chap. XIX, p. 34.

3

married Christians to know that adultery, abortion, and dishonesty with the spouse are immoral.

It is true that the virtuous man, including the man who leads a life of marital virtue, does not have to be a theologian. But he does have to think; his virtue must grow within a theological vision of life. If he has no idealism, then his virtue will be mere satisfied rule-keeping — the kind of religion which Jesus so strongly denounced (Mt 6:2–4; Mk 13:38–40). Nietzsche was contemptuous of the virtuous man precisely because the Christianity of nineteenth-century Germany presented as its highest ideal the man who kept the rules by avoiding sin. To be a Christian, a man must have more than a rule of correct behavior. He must understand the true significance which the mystery of Christ holds for himself and the world around him. Such an understanding is sometimes not achieved by "religious" people because it is a human characteristic that man finds it difficult to maintain his relationship to God without reducing morality to a systematic list of behavioral rules.[2] Moral life becomes ritualistic, then irrelevant, when a formalized list of do's and don'ts becomes the warp and woof of a good life. To be a true Christian, a man must relate the reality of Christ to his daily life within some vision, some world picture. If he is married, the Christian must have some understanding of how his marital condition is the daily vehicle by which he participates in creation and redemption. A theologian the married Christian does not need to be; but he needs a theology of marriage. He needs a vision of marriage in Christ which will motivate him to daily make his life a sacramental act of the Christian Church.

Historical Obstacles to the Development of a Theology of Marriage

Although some writers have made significant contributions to the development of a contemporary theology of marriage,[3] the Christian today is still struggling to formulate and develop the basic principles of such a theology. Certain historical developments have impeded this work. It is important to appreciate the factors which have mitigated the full flowering of a theology of marriage because their historical residue is still frequently found in contemporary thought.

---

[2] For an excellent analysis of this tendency, see Marc Oraison, Introduction to Love or Constraint? (New York: P. J. Kenedy, 1959).

[3] See, for example, the books by Kerns, Oraison, and Schillebeeckx listed in the bibliography of Part I.

The major obstacle to the development of a theology of marriage in recent centuries has been the generally static and legalistic condition of moral theological thought. Moral theology did not really develop as a separate branch of theological study until near the end of the medieval period. In the fourteenth and fifteenth centuries the theologian who specialized in the morality of human acts came on the scene. He soon developed an independent science, with its own tools and sources. Concurrent to the development of moral theology, Western ethical, political, social, and economic thought was increasingly characterized by a pragmatic and self-centered philosophy of man. Influential thinkers in different fields, such as Machiavelli, John Locke, and Adam Smith espoused such a philosophy. Man was told that he should act for practical here-and-now goals, and that his action should be rooted in an enlightened self-interest. Catholic moral theologians did not consciously accept these ideas, but Western civilization became so imbued with such thoughts that the moral theologian could not escape their influence. They were part of his intellectual milieu. Moral theology came to be a practical or applied science in which the self-interest of the individual soul rather than the social consciousness of the Gospel came to be the ideal. The Christian ideal of a man aspiring to be like the Heavenly Father (Mt 5:48) was obscured in the moral tracts which were extended lists of the minimums needed to avoid sin. The typical moral manual came very close to espousing a form of enlightened self-interest in the emphasis given to individual, spiritual development while neglecting the outward, turning love of God in the neighbor which is the dominant New Testament theme (Mt 22:34–40; Jn 15:12; 1 Cor 13:1–13; 1 Jn 4:7–12).

Most of the writing about marriage in recent centuries has been done by the moralists. They frequently pictured marital life as a satisfactory but inferior means of personal salvation for the spouse who kept the rules. If the married person avoided sins of adultery, contraception, and divorce, he could slip into heaven. This negative, legalistic, and self-centered way of looking at marriage came to be reflected in the pulpit and popular religious writings.[4] It certainly failed to stir up in the mind of the average Christian any inspiring vision of his marital potentialities.

---

[4] In the light of these comments the reader may find it helpful to evaluate: C. H. Doyle, *Cana Is Forever* (Tarrytown: Nugent Press, 1949); W. Handren, *No Longer Two* (Westminster: Newman, 1955); G. Kelly, *The Catholic Marriage Manual* (New York: Random House, 1958); W. Lynch, *A Marriage Manual For Catholics* (New York: Trident Press, 1964); and V. Nugent, (ed.), *Christian Marriage* (New York: St. John's University Studies, 1961).

At best, it produced some satisfied rule-keeping.

The failure of moral theology to make marriage theologically intelligible was accompanied by a similar failure on the part of those sacramental theologians who wrote of marital union. In recent centuries most Catholics have tended to think of a sacrament exclusively in terms of its grace-giving qualities. "Marriage is a sacrament because it gives me grace to carry out the duties of my state in life" is not an uncommon idea. And it is a correct idea. But, as a living definition of the sacrament, it is wanting. The spiritual shower or grace digestion approach to the sacrament of marriage left most married Christians with only the vaguest idea of their role in the redemptive work of Christ.

In every age of its history the Church has had to contend with a dualist-spiritualist tendency which led some people to believe that sex is evil. In rejecting Gnosticism, Manichaeism, Albigensianism, Catharism, Jansenism, and other dualistic theories, the Church was upholding its faith in God's revelation that sexual love is one of the means by which man participates in the mysteries of creation and redemption. Even with this consistent upholding of the goodness of sex a residue of anti-sexual spiritualism can still be found in the thinking of some Christians. Inasmuch as a perverted view of sex makes a vital theology of marriage impossible, this obstacle is a difficult one.

Still, another obstacle in the way of developing a theology of marriage has been the tendency of some writers to maximize the importance of consecrated virginity by minimizing the value of marriage within the Christian scheme of life. This tendency has been present almost from the beginning of the Christian Church and probably results from the difficulty which the followers of Christ have had in expressing their appreciation of virginity. To understand why a Christian cherishes virginity presupposes a belief in the Incarnation, whereas the holiness of marriage as a natural institution can be explained without reference to the Incarnation. It is only when a man believes that "the Word became flesh and dwelt among us" (Jn 1:14) that he can seek to give an "undivided devotion to the Lord" (1 Cor 7:35) as a virginal instrument of the humanity of Christ. That "Christ Jesus, who, though he was in form of God, did not count equality with God a thing to be grasped, but emptied himself, taking the form of a servant, being born in the likeness of men" (Phil 2:5-7) is a fact of faith which staggers the human imagination. To the unbeliever, such a belief must seem "foolishness" (1 Cor 1:24), and its application in a life of virginity must seem unnatural

and irrational. As an application of and participation in the love which
is at the root of the Incarnation, virginity makes no sense outside of the
mystery of Christ. The apostle Paul attempted to explain this to the
Corinthians by explaining the totality with which the virgin can dedicate
himself to the service of the whole Christian community: "the un-
married man is anxious about the affairs of the Lord" (1 Cor 7:32).
The Apostles did not disparage marriage as a unique form of Christian
mystery (Eph 5:32); rather, they tried to show the true basis for Christian virginity as a union with Christ (whom they believed lived now
in the Church) by which the virgin could serve the cause of redemption
in widest possible community.

Post-apostolic Christians, however, were often unable to explain the
incarnational basis for virginity and sometimes attempted to build a
false apologetic by downgrading marriage. As early as the second century,
anti-marriage writings were circulating within the Church. The most
popular of these were the Protoevangelium of James and the Gospel of
Pseudo-Matthew. These writings consisted of apocryphal legends about
Christ. Some parts of these stories were aimed at refuting the attacks
on the virgin birth which were circulating among second-century Roman
and Jewish writers. The Protoevangelium of James tried to uphold Mary's
virginity by denying her marriage to Joseph. Mary is described as having
been presented in the Temple at the age of three in order to consecrate
her virginity to the Lord. The author of this story was not deterred by
the fact that such a ceremony could never have happened in Israel.
Joseph was pictured as an old man who was incapable of marriage; he
agrees merely to become the protector of Mary. This is in flat contradic-
tion to the canonical Gospels of Matthew and Luke in which Joseph
is pictured as a vigorous, hardworking carpenter who is already betrothed
(betrothal was a non-consummated marriage) to Mary when the virgin
bride experiences the annunciation. All too frequently the apocryphal
gospels attempted to defend Mary's virginity by denying her marriage.

In later centuries the tendency to explain virginity by attacking marriage spread. St. Cyril of Jerusalem had to warn that "you who are so
excited about virginity must be careful not to attack those who are
married."[5] The tracts of many medieval theologians sometimes treated

---

[5] Catechism 4. Cyril's contemporary, St. Amphilocius of Iconium, attacked the
same situation in a passage which sets forth the esteem in which the early Christians
held marriage: "Virginity is honorable . . . a means by which man enters into the
bridal chamber with Christ the bridegroom . . . but marriage is also honorable in
everyone who undertakes it. It is the greatest of God's earthly gifts. It is a tree from

marriage not only as a less perfect way of Christian life by comparison with virginity, and in this they were correct, but also as a mere concession to human frailty. Even today one meets Christians with the opinion that marriage is for second-rate Christians.

This tendency to stress virginity by downgrading marriage is especially paradoxical when one remembers that the Scriptures, many writers, and even the prayer which is recited at the consecration of the virgin, picture the virgin as aspiring to the holiness represented in marriage. Christian virginity needs no false apologetics, especially not one constructed at the expense of marriage. Its importance is too firmly rooted in Scripture (Mt 19:11–12; 1 Cor 7:7) to need a false defense.

Still another historical cause for the slow way in which a theology of marriage has been developed has been the general reluctance of the layman to express his thoughts on the subject. This has been less true in the Eastern Churches where many theologians are either married laymen or married clerics. In the Western Churches, Catholic and Reformation, most theologians have been clerics until recent years, and among Catholics few clerics are married. As a result, the actual experience of marriage has been a neglected source of information vital to the development of a theology of marriage. Many married Catholics complain that most of the theological writing on marriage they experience has an "unrealistic" tone to it — the language and feelings expressed is not that of a living knowledge of marriage.

Will the twentieth century witness the development of a theology of marriage? It is possible. An awareness of the social implications of Christianity is growing;[6] less emphasis is being given to rules of behavior as moral theologians strive to build systems based on love;[7] a vital sacra-

---

which comes great fruit; it is the root of virginity. . . . Marriage is the gift bestowed for the increase of the world, for the comfort of man, to paint the image of God in man. It is blessed by God, and he further honored it in order that he might become man. . . . I in no way desire to contribute to a conflict between virginity and marriage for we admire both. One completes the other. The Providence of God has decreed that one must not be placed against the other. The true service of God embraces both. Without love of God neither marriage nor virginity is holy." *In Honor of Virginity, Marriage, and Widowhood.*

[6] See, for example, K. Rahner, *Christian in the Market Place* (New York: Sheed and Ward, 1966).

[7] See G. Gilleman, *The Primacy of Charity in Moral Theology* (Westminster: Newman Press, 1961); T. Heath, *In the Face of Anguish* (New York: Sheed and Ward, 1966); C. Spicq, *Charity and Liberty in the New Testament* (Staten Island: Alba House, 1966).

mental theology is growing;[8] the layman is no longer content to chew silently on stones when he longs for bread. However, in recent years, the intense discussion of birth control among Catholic theologians has itself presented a new obstacle to the development of a theology of marriage. Much has been written about the nature of sexual love, but the framework of the discussion has been too frequently narrowed by the interest in "solving" the birth limitation controversy.[9] Pope Paul VI described this problem as one which "touches the mainsprings of human life,"[10] and there can be no doubt that the frank and open analysis of it among Catholic scholars has contributed to a deeper understanding of both marriage and the Church. But it is to be hoped that future analyses of marriage by theologians will broaden to the point where all the major concerns, problems, opportunities, and common experiences will be worthy of detailed analysis from a Christian perspective.

---

[8] See B. Cooke, *Christian Sacraments and Christian Personality* (New York: Holt, Rinehart, and Winston, 1965); K. Rahner, *The Church and the Sacraments* (New York: Herder and Herder, 1963); E. Schillebeeckx, *Christ: The Sacrament of the Encounter with God* (New York: Sheed and Ward, 1963); J. Schanz, *The Sacraments of Life and Worship* (Milwaukee: The Bruce Publishing Company, 1966).

[9] For the author's opinion, see "The Issue Revisited; the Problems Go Beyond Birth Control," *Ave Maria*, Vol. 102, No. 6 (Aug. 7, 1965) and three book reviews in *Commonweal*, Vol. LXXXII, No. 12 (June 11, 1965), p. 389.

[10] Talk of June 23, 1964, A.A.S. 56.

CHAPTER 2

MARRIAGE IS A SANCTIFICATION
OF HUMAN LIFE

The Natural and Supernatural Life

Many religious and theological books build elaborate themes around the distinction between nature and grace, between creation and redemption, between nature and supernature. The distinction is valid, but improper use is sometimes made of it. This confusion is particularly apparent in some commentaries on marriage. Divorce, contraception, and polygamy are sometimes denounced as being based on "naturalistic" views of marriage. Contrasts are sometimes drawn between natural and supernatural marriage as if they were contradictory realities. These authors frequently intend to make a valid point, but their terminology is most unfortunate. Marriage is a natural institution; that it is also a Christian sacrament in no way detracts from its natural holiness. To describe an evil in marriage as natural or naturalistic is to place a very serious obstacle in the way of understanding Christian marriage. The bishops of the Second Vatican Council described marital love as one which is "eminently human,"[1] and the Christian must seek to understand why this is so.

One cannot appreciate the Christian sacramentality of marriage until he has developed an awareness of the nature of marital love in God's plan for creation. A statement prepared by one of the commissions at the First Vatican Council noted that "it is unfortunate that some men think the religion of Christ reduces the dignity of human nature because it is a supernatural religion."[2] The life given to man by Christ (Jn 20:31) is certainly distinguishable from the natural life of man (2 Cor 5:17), but it is also true that the former builds on and perfects the latter (Eph 1:9-10).

Grace will not cure cancer or schizophrenia, but it will make the cancerous person or schizophrenic, a "partaker of the divine nature" (2 Pet 1:4), while leaving him still a man. Unquestionably, there are some Catholics who fail to understand redemption because they do not appreciate the truth of creation. Theirs is a supernatural religion, but by supernatural they mean it hangs in a void rather than in the natural world where the Incarnation placed it (Phil 2:1-11). They forget that "nature should remain nature for the sake of grace and yet be grasped by the Christian as an intrinsic element in the single object willed by God when he willed man as his beloved in his Son."[3]

Before an examination of marriage as a sacrament of the New Law is attempted, marital love must be studied from the viewpoint of natural creation. What did the Creator intend when he made man a thinking, sexual being? If one can achieve some insight into the divine will on marriage, he will be in a better position to understand why Christ found marital love a particularly fitting instrument of redemption. This is why this chapter, and the subsequent one, are concerned only with the natural foundation of marital holiness.

The Origin of Marriage in the Judeo-Christian Tradition

It is obvious that marriage is not Jewish or Christian in origin. The permanent union of a man and woman in family life existed long before

---

[1] The Pastoral Constitution on the Church in the Modern World, art. 49.

[2] Schema of the Dogmatic Constitution on Catholic Doctrine. Because the Italian Revolution interrupted the First Vatican Council, the schema was never formally adopted.

[3] Karl Rahner, Theological Investigations (Baltimore: Helicon Press, 1961), Vol. I, p. 317.

Israel. But the Christian and Jew believe that revelation does tell the believer something about the origin of marriage and its relation to the divine will. In the first three chapters of Genesis the ancient Israelites wrote down what they believed about God's creation of the universe. These words also express the belief of Christians (Heb 1:1; Rom 9:4-5). These three chapters form a kind of prologue to the whole of salvation history, but they are especially valuable in setting up themes on marriage which are carried all the way through the Old and New Testaments.

One passage particularly illustrates Judeo-Christian thinking about the origin of marriage:

> Then the Lord God said, "It is not good that man should be alone; I will make him a helper fit for him." . . . So the Lord God caused a deep sleep to fall upon the man, and while he slept took one of his ribs and closed up its place with flesh, and the rib which the Lord God had taken from the man he made into a woman and brought her to the man. Then the man said, "This at last is the bone of my bones and flesh of my flesh; and she shall be called woman because she was taken out of man." Therefore, a man leaves his father and his mother and cleaves to his wife, and they shall become one flesh (Gen 2:18-24).

The men who wrote these words many years ago were not anthropologists. It is unthinkable that they intended to convey some scientific data about the marriage practices of primitive man. What they expressed was their faith in the fact that God is the ultimate explanation of man's existence and a belief that man's marital life is bound up with the truth of creation. In other words, the ancient Israelites believed that marriage is more than a social institution devised by man for his own convenience; to them, marriage was an integral part of human existence as the Creator intended it to be.[4]

Starting with the publication of *Das Mutterrecht* by Bachafen in Germany in 1861, a great debate over the existence of marriage among primitive peoples has long been going on.[5] But this is an anthropological question, not a theological problem. The Christian is not so much concerned with what ancient men did as with what he should do in his life. In the story of man's creation, as male and female dedicated to a complete union of one flesh, the Christian finds a statement of his

---

[4] "Let this remain the unchanged and unmoveable foundation: Matrimony is not the institution of man; nor did man restore it; it is of God." Pope Pius XI, *Casti Connubii*, A.A.S. 22 (1930).

[5] The weight of scientific evidence today favors the existence of monogamous marriage in primitive society. See R. Mohr, "The Primitive Races," in von Hornstein and Faller, *Sex-Love-Marriage*, cited in the bibliography, Chap. 26.

belief that marriage holds a high place in the Creator's plan for human existence. This is why Pope Pius XI spoke of the "divine origin" of marriage.[6] Pope Leo XIII was even more explicit when he wrote that "union in marriage is not the invention of man; it is from God Himself, the supreme author of nature."[7]

Marriage Makes Man Holy

The second and later interpretation of creation in Genesis runs from 1:1–2:3. It dates from about the year 950 B.C. and reflects a much better organized religious thought than the more primitive account quoted earlier. It probably was written down by a group of Hebrew priests or theologians. Although different from the creation story woven around Adam and Eve, this "priestly" account also reflects the Jewish belief in the connection between marriage and the purpose of man's existence:

> Then God said, "Let us make man in our image, after our likeness; and let them have dominion over the fish of the sea, and over the birds of the air, and over the cattle, and over all the earth, and over every creeping thing that creeps upon the earth." So God created man in his own image, in the image of God he created him; male and female he created them. And God blessed them, and God said to them: "Be fruitful, and multiply, and fill the earth and subdue it;" . . . and it was so. And God saw everything that he had made, and behold it was very good (Gen 1:26–31).

It is obvious from this text that man is a very unusual creature. Other beings have existence from God, as does man. Other beings experience the thrill of life, as does man. Other beings are sexual, as is man. Yet man is singled out from the rest of creation and described as being in the "image of God." The source of this divine likeness in man is frequently missed by writers who dwell on the "spirituality" of human beings.[8] The text emphasizes the sexuality of man: "So God created man in his own image, in the image of God he created him, male and female he created them" (Gen 1:27). Of course, the Jews did not think of God as a sexual being, but human sexuality is somehow linked to the divine

---

[6] Encyclical Letter, Casti Connubii, supra, n. 4.

[7] Encyclical Letter to the Bishops of Piedmont, Ci Siamo, June 1, 1889, A.S.S. 22.

[8] In Christian literature, the "spiritualist" interpretation of man's likeness to God had its beginnings in the neo-Platonic third-century writings of Origen. In the Dialogue with Heraclides the great Alexandrian father wrote: "He created man in the image of God. Moses knew that this likeness to God was immaterial, superior to any bodily being."

likeness in man. In commenting on these verses Gerhard von Rad has observed:

> By God's will, man was not created alone, but designated for the "thou" of the other sex. The idea of man . . . finds its full meaning not in the male alone but in man and woman.[9]

That the scriptural text expresses such a belief is apparent from a reading of the Talmud. The section of the Talmud dealing with marriage is entitled "Kiddushin," a word derived from *Kodosh*: something holy. Marriage has, as its purpose, sanctification, the building of God's image in husband and wife. This is reflected in the very words by which a Jewish man marries his bride. *Hare et Mekudeshet Li*, he says to her: "Be thou made holy in me."

But how is marriage the source of man's sanctification? Notice that it is not man alone who is in the image of God — or woman. Gen 2:18–24 shows the incompleteness of male or female alone. It is man and woman joined together in a union of mutual fruitful dedication, a union rooted in their sexual difference, which constitutes such a dramatic image of God in creation.

To the Jew, God is pre-eminently the Creator; and the ancient Israelites thought of marriage as a participation in the mystery of creation. The sexuality of the male or female is useless in itself, but when two sexually differentiated human beings form a human community, a new form of creative potentiality comes into existence.

In one sense, marriage enables man to participate in creation through the begetting of new human life and development of that life in the familial unit. The sexual activity of all animals is such a participation in the mystery of creation. Yet, it is the union of man and woman which is blessed for its fruitfulness in some special and singular way (Gen 1:28). This is because the Jews knew God to be a person, a free and intelligent being who uses his creative powers knowingly and not from blind impulse. Of all the sexual beings he created, only man reflects the intelligence and freedom of God in the use of creative power. Man alone can consciously choose to participate in God's act of creation through sex; in him sex is more than an impulse.[10]

When marriage is described as procreative, its most obvious meaning is that through marital love human life is brought into existence and

---

[9] *Genesis* (London: SCM Press, 1956), p. 58.

[10] "The particular and unique nature of the marital contract makes it something which is entirely different from the instinctual union of the lower animals; the latter does not involve reason or free choice." *Casti Connubii, supra*, n. 4.

brought to maturity. However, marriage is procreative in a different but equally profound sense. The Adam and Eve account of creation pictures the male as incomplete and lonely (Gen 2:18–20). Man, complete and whole, is not created until male and female come together in a union of one flesh which makes them a whole being. When such a union takes place, man recognizes his wholeness: "This at last is the bone of my bones and flesh of my flesh" (Gen 1:23). Marriage reflects the creative life of God because within this union man actually is empowered to complete his own creation; he makes himself fully human by finding in his spouse the remedy for his own inadequacies as a male or female. Thus man achieves holiness, a likeness to the Creator, by procreating his own human condition. This is why he "leaves his father and mother and cleaves to his wife, and they become one flesh" (Gen 2:24).

The Christian does not think of God only in the light of creation. He believes that Jesus has given man an insight into the very nature of God. Jesus reveals not only what God has done, but what God is. This is what sets Christianity apart in the history of religion, Christ's teaching on God and the moral consequences he draws from it. Later generations of Christians called his teaching the "Trinity," the belief that God is Father, Son, and Spirit — an eternal union of unmeasuring and un-measurable love. In the words of the apostle John, the Christian believes that "God is Love" (1 Jn 4:8). Marriage establishes man in the image and likeness of God inasmuch as it reflects the Trinitarian existence. Obviously the Genesis text would not contain such an idea. But the "love" by which a Christian defines God is also the only word which adequately expresses his idea of marriage.[11] In marriage, the fundamental human longing for communion finds its natural culmination, for it is only in marriage that one human being says to another: "I give myself to you completely." Thus marriage is a true likeness to the divine life of unstinting self-giving found in the created universe. It is complete and unending self-giving which makes God what he is. The Christian believes that man can share in the love life of God in marriage. Thus he achieves sanctification.

The Pre-Christian Sacramental Character of Marriage

If marriage is a reflection of God's life, it must also be true that every marriage sanctifies human life. Pope Leo XIII wrote that:

---

[11] See Chap. 4, the section entitled "Marriage as a Participation in Christ's Law of Love."

God is the author of marriage. From the moment of man's creation marriage foreshadowed the Incarnation. Therefore it is holy and religious; this is not incidental but innate, not introduced by men but by nature. Therefore Our Predecessors, Innocent III and Honorius III, affirmed that the "sacrament of marriage exists among believers and unbelievers," that is, among Christians and non-Christians alike. In summary, marriage is holy in its essence, in its nature, and by itself.[12]

The application of the word sacarment (sacramentum) to every marriage was so startling that several of Pope Leo's translators were unwilling to put his phrasing into the vernacular languages. But the encyclical expresses the authentic belief of Catholics; the Pope pointedly indicated this by citing two earlier Popes. Christians believe that God, in the act of ordaining the evolution of the human race as male and female and willing marital love as an image of his own life and existence, made marriage a sacramental act. This is true even outside of Christ's redemptive act. In the phrase of Pope Pius XI, the married couple are "the instruments of God's almighty power."[13] It is this pre-Christian sacramental character which makes marriage an especially fitting instrument for the redemptive power which Jesus exercises in his Body, the Church. This is why Pope Leo called marriage a foreshadowing of the Incarnation. It is a theme which will be more fully developed in Chapter 4.

---

[12] Encyclical Letter Arcanum Divinae Sapientiac, A.S.S., 12 (1879–1880).
[13] Casti Connubii, supra, n. 4.

CHAPTER 3

MARRIAGE IS THE
COMPLETION OF MAN

The Meaning of Two Become One Flesh

What is marriage? Friedrich Nietzsche defined it as "the will of two to create the one who is greater than they who create it."[1] The essence of marriage is two persons seeking to form a more perfect life through their giving of themselves totally to each other. In the words of the ancient Jewish text "a man leaves his father and his mother and cleaves to his wife, and they become one flesh" (Gen 2:24). So accurate, from a Christian perspective, is this description of marriage that when the Pharisees sought to test Jesus' teaching on marriage he based his answer squarely on the Genesis text:[2] "Have you not read that he who made them from

---

[1] *Thus Spoke Zarathustra*, Part I, Discourse XX.

[2] Jesus used the Genesis text here to support his teaching on the unity and indissolubility of marriage. His interpretation of the text had contemporary support in the Samaritan and Greek (Septuagint) texts of Gen 2:24. These texts rendered "they become one flesh" as "these two shall become one."

the beginning made them male and female, and said, 'For this reason a man shall leave his father and mother and be joined to his wife, and the two shall become one! So they are no longer two but one" (Mt 19:4–5). Two have become one — an expression of the heart of marital love.

Marriage is more than an agreement between a man and woman to live together; more than a mutual exchange of promises of support and comfort; more than an agreement to observe the civil and ecclesiastical laws of marriage; more than a promise to help each other achieve union with God. A marriage may involve all of these intermingled agreements, but none of them define marriage. Only two seeking to become perfectly one flesh with each other do that. The Hebrew word for flesh denotes a complete union, a complete being. It carries connotations for the unity of the couple's families, but primarily it refers to continuing creation of the fullness of human life which takes place when man and woman marry. Their union is based on the incomplete sexuality of the male or female, a lack of wholeness which is remedied only in a union of total commitment between them. This incompleteness of each sex alone is apparent in the physical dimension, but it runs deeply into the psychological order. "Then the Lord God said, 'It is not good that man should be alone; I will make him a helper fit for him'" (Gen 2:18).[3] The Israelites who wrote these words were not psychologists, but they recognized that the marital union fills a physical-psychological void existing in male and female alone. They believed that in marriage man procreates the fullness of human life. A distinguished psychologist has expressed a similar thought in these words:

> A wife and her husband can complement each other's activities. . . .
> As they make their own satisfactions mutually dependent upon each
> other, they increase their very capacity for happiness . . . there is more
> stimulation; one takes over where the other leaves off, and many previ-
> ously unnoticed details of our lives develop new emotional significance
> . . . ideally, the intimacy of marriage offers us the opportunity of freeing
> ourselves, and simultaneously enjoying an acceptance — in fact an admira-
> tion and love — of that self.[4]

The fathers of the Second Vatican Council described marital love as

---

[3] The phrase "a helper fit for him" would better be translated "corresponding to him." See Speiser, Genesis, The Anchor Bible (New York: Doubleday and Co., 1964), p. 17. This translation would more effectively bring out the complementariness of masculinity and femininity.

[4] Allan Fromme, Sex and Marriage (New York: Barnes and Noble, 1965), p. 36.

one which is "eminently human . . . since it is directed from one person to another through an affection of the will . . . this love the Lord has judged worthy of special gifts, healing, perfecting, and exalting gifts of grace and charity."[5]

Marriage as the Totality of Human Nature

The Judeo-Christian ideal of marriage involves a complete giving by the parties in a personal union which transcends the individuality of either partner. Thus is the full human person of the one flesh created. This new and perfected human life consists of the merger of complementary masculinity and femininity as these exist in the individual persons. In the Adam and Eve story there is an incompleteness in man which is remedied through his union with woman; the complete human person consists of the male and female pledged to complementary union.

In a most obvious sense the sex organs of male and female find their functional purpose in union with another person of the opposite sex. The construction of the male penis, the method by which the spermatozoa are produced and carried through the urethra, the expulsion of the seminal fluid from the tip of the penis: this is of no functional value to man except in coitus. The sperm itself is useless unless placed in the body of a woman where it can fertilize the egg. The female vagina is structured to receive the male penis, to serve as the passage for the menstrual discharge if the egg has not been fertilized, and to be the birth canal by which the conceived child will pass from the body of the woman. The egg has no value if it is not fertilized. A woman's breasts find their purpose in the feeding of a child born of the union and in foreplay of the marital embrace.

Male and female incompleteness goes beyond these obvious physical inadequacies of each sex alone. We commonly speak of masculine and feminine characteristics. These characteristics are partly rooted in the physical-psychological makeup of male and female. Historical factors which have helped to mold the family structure, environmental influences in a given society, and the need for a division of labor in the familial unit have also helped to develop these characteristics by conditioning people to expect certain role-playing from each sex. It is also true that no male is entirely masculine and no woman possesses all the characteristics of the female per-

---

[5] *The Pastoral Constitution on the Church in the Modern World*, art. 49.

sonality perfectly. Sometimes, a normal male will follow a pattern of conduct which is typically feminine. While all of these considerations are relevant, masculinity and femininity are existent realities having at least some basis in the physical-psychological makeup of the man and woman.

One example of masculinity and femininity is the complementary roles of paternity and maternity. By paternity, one means the exteriorly active agent of generation. Biologically, it is the male who must come into the female before new life can be conceived. On another level, before the new life of the one flesh in the marital union comes into existence, the man is expected to pursue and actively woo the female. The man is also expected to take the exteriorly active role in promoting the life of the family by providing for its physical well-being and defending it from outside danger.

Maternity is characterized by a role which is complementary to that of paternity. It has often been described as a passive role, but this term conveys an improper sense of inertia. Maternity would better be described as the interiorly active agency of generation. Biologically, it is the woman who opens herself to receive the man; if conception takes place she holds and nourishes the new life within her body until it can exist independently of her. The woman turns within to make herself attractive in order that she will be wooed into new familial life. She strengthens the internal life of the family by using the support and protection provided by the husband to build a vital home life. Only in marriage are these complementary roles possible of fulfillment.

The complementariness of man and woman might be described in other ways. Many people speak of feminine intuition. This is a closeness to the way of nature and an immersion in the fabric of life which gives woman a subjective feel for the values and needs of life. The male is often described as being objectively logical, that is, having a certain detachment from nature and mastery over life processes. These descriptions refer only to tendencies which do not exist perfectly in any man or woman. But to the extent that they do exist in a given couple, they are complementary.

It is by coming together in marital union that man and woman, through the exercise of their complementary roles, create the full human person. This is why the Old Testament describes a wife as the "crown of her husband" (Prov 12:4), and it is why Adam said of Eve: "This at last is bone of my bones and flesh of my flesh" (Gen 2:23).

Indissolubility of the Marital Union

When a man and woman give themselves to each other in a union so complete that they are called one flesh, there is a totality of commitment to each other. This is why Christians describe marriage as an indissoluble or permanent union. Some of the man-made civil and social consequences of marriage are subject to change and destruction, but the new life created by marital love is meant to continue as long as husband and wife exist. When some Pharisees sought to test Jesus' understanding of the law which allowed a man to put away his wife, he answered by pointing out that a man leaves his parents to cleave to his wife and become one flesh with her (cf. Mt 19:5). Because they have become one, a new human life, their union should not be destroyed. "So they are no longer two but one. What therefore God has joined together, let no man put asunder" (Mt 19:6).

In giving practical advice to the Christians of Corinth, the apostle Paul applied this teaching of Jesus: "A wife is bound to her husband as long as he lives. If the husband dies, she is free to be married to whom she wishes, only in the Lord" (1 Cor 7:39). Jesus himself bluntly stated this teaching: "Every one who divorces his wife and marries another commits adultery, and he who marries a woman divorced from her husband commits adultery" (Lk 16:18) . . . "whoever divorces his wife and marries another, commits adultery against her; and if she divorces her husband and marries another, she commits adultery" (Mk 10:11–12).

Christian practice in the question of remarriage following a civil divorce has sometimes varied in the interpretation of indissolubility; this variation will be examined more closely in Chapter 15 of Part IV. The Roman Catholic position is defined by the Council of Florence: "it is not permitted to contract marriage with another because the marital bond is perpetual."[6] However, the purpose of the present chapter is not to examine application and practice of indissolubility but to understand its reasons.

One of the historical reasons for indissolubility was emphasized by Pope Pius XII when he noted that in societies not recognizing marriage as a permanent union the "dignity of woman has been outraged, injured and trampled underfoot."[7] It is probable that one of the reasons that the Adam and Eve story was included in the Sacred Text was to dis-

---

[6] Denz. 1327.
[7] "Talk to Newlyweds," April 29, 1942, A.A.S., 35.

courage the Israelites from mistreating their wives through bills of divorce. It is true that the Mosaic Law did eventually permit bills of divorce (Dt 24:1-4), but Jesus attributes this to man's inhumanity to women: "From your hardness of heart Moses allowed you to divorce your wives, but from the beginning it was not so" (Mt 19:8).

Another important reason for indissolubility is the parental work of procreating children to the fullness of human maturity in a stable family life.

However, the heart of indissolubility is not to be found in historical or educational considerations but in the relationship of permanence to the perfection of marital love. The Good Samaritan gives himself to his neighbor, the teacher to his student, the politician to his people. Yet, however good these acts of unselfish love, they are not comparable to the self-dedication with which a husband and wife give themselves to each other and their children in an enduring marital union of body, mind, and spirit. The union of one flesh is not a passing contact, not a fleeting touching. It is only when a man and woman say to each other "I commit myself to you totally" that there is marital love. The one flesh is a new creature which is capable of growth over a lifetime. As the bishops of Second Vatican wrote:

> A man and woman . . . by the marriage covenant of conjugal love "are no longer two, but one flesh" (Mt 19:6) render mutual help and service to each other through an intimate union of their persons and their actions. Through this intimate union, they experience the meaning of their oneness and attain to it with growing perfection day by day. As a mutual gift of two persons, this intimate union, as well as the good of the children, imposes total fidelity on the spouses and argues for an unbreakable oneness between them.[8]

Marital love is the work of a lifetime, a lifetime of self-giving and self-fulfillment. This requires the constant development of the channels of communication between husband and wife. As they grow ever closer in understanding, the opportunity for love increases. Indissolubility is not a burden, but a challenge to build the total human person, a challenge to love.

---

[8] *Supra*, n. 5, art. 48.

CHAPTER 4

MARRIAGE IS A SACRAMENT
OF THE NEW LAW

Man communicates by signs. The Christian believes that God has revealed himself in the unfolding drama of saving history by means of
signs. Man does not know God directly but only through signs. "It is
appropriate to Sacred Scripture," wrote St. Thomas Aquinas, "to picture
divine things under the similitude of bodily things. God provides for
all according to their nature; it is natural to man to know things through
sensible things."[1]

Jesus as a Sacramental Sign

The Gospels describe the life of Jesus as a sign to man: "Now Jesus
did many other signs in the presence of the disciples, which are not
written in this book, but these [signs] are written that you may believe

---

[1] *Summa of Theology*, I, Q. 1, Art. 9.

that Jesus is the Christ, the Son of God, and that believing you may
have life in his name" (Jn 20:30–31). Jesus' life of service to the neighbor
in need, to the sick, to the hungry, to the ignorant, to the sinner — this
is the most powerful sign that "he who loves is born of God . . . for
God is love" (1 Jn 4:7–8).

The Christian believes that Jesus Christ is the one great sign by which
God is primarily known.

> Philip said to him, "Lord show us the Father, and we shall be satisfied."
> Jesus said to him, "Have I been with you so long, and yet you do not
> know me, Philip? He who has seen me has seen the Father" (Jn 14:8–9).

The apostle John wrote of the thrill experienced by his disciples in
knowing God in the physical sign which is Jesus:

> That which was from the beginning, which we have heard, which we
> have seen with our eyes, which we have looked upon and touched with
> our hands — the life which was made manifest, and we saw it, and
> testify to it, and proclaim to you the eternal life which was with the
> Father and was made manifest to us — that which we have seen and
> heard we proclaim also to you (1 Jn 1:1–3).

But Jesus does more than represent the divine; he also brings it to
man. He is a sign of life who brings life: "come to me that you may
have life" (Jn 5:40). Jesus is a sacrament, the great sacrament, because
he represents and causes God's life in those who come to him.

The Actions of the Church as Acts of Jesus, the Great Sacrament

When Jesus no longer walked among his friends and followers, were
they left without further experience of sacrament? The apostle Paul, who
had not known Jesus before the Ascension, expressed the conviction in
his letters that he now experienced the reality of Christ. "Now you are
the body of Christ" (1 Cor 12:27), he wrote to the Christians at Corinth.[2]
At the time of his conversion, Paul was asked "Saul, Saul, why do you
persecute me?" And he said, "Who are you, Lord?" "I am Jesus, whom
you are persecuting" (Acts 9:4–5). It was the Christians whom Paul
had been dragging off to prison (Acts 8:3), but it was Jesus whom Paul
had been persecuting. In their common faith (Eph 4:1–5), their love of
God in neighbor (Gal 5:14), their service of each other (1 Cor 12:25)
and in their good works (Phil 2:13) Paul sees the Christians as consti-

---

[2] For a clear explanation of Paul's meaning see M. Lane, S.J., "The Body of Christ
in First Corinthians," *The Bible Today*, I (Feb., 1964), 650.

tuting Christ. Together, the Christians work to establish "the stature of the fulness of Christ" (Eph 4:13).

In his letters Paul describes some of the things which the Christians, the body of Christ, do together. They eat a common bread as a sign of unity (1 Cor 12:17–22); the bread actually makes them one (1 Cor 10:17). They wash new members of the community as a sign of their death and resurrection in Christ (Rom 6:3–7); because of this baptism the new members have actually put on Christ (Gal 3:27). They lay hands on the leaders of the community (1 Tim 4:14) as a sign of their appointment to teach; the grace of God is imparted to those on whom hands have been laid (2 Tim 1:6). In addition to these symbolic-effective (and therefore sacramental) acts of the body of Christ St. Paul sees one more — marriage. The Christians marry, a sign of the love existing between Christ and the Church (Eph 5:25). But marriage not only symbolizes the unity of Christ and the Church; it is also a "great mystery, and I take it to mean Christ and the Church" (Eph 5:32). Thus marriage is one of the sacramental means by which Christ acts through his Church.

Pope Leo I once said in the fourth century that "what once was seen in Christ our Redeemer is now seen in the sacraments of the Church."[3] Marriage is a Christian sacrament because it is a redemptive action of the body of Christ. Jesus lives again in the Christian love of husband and wife.

Jesus Bears Witness to the Intrinsic Holiness of Marriage

When the Christian Church reflected on its own actions, and concluded to the sacramental nature of marriage, it was in no way depreciating the innate holiness of marriage described in Chapter 2. When it described Jesus as "instituting" the sacrament of matrimony, the Church meant that an already existing cause of holiness has received a new redemptive purpose. St. Albert the Great once described marriage as having several inaugurations;[4] marriage as a Christian redemptive institution is a perfection of the procreative institution which the Creator established.[5] Indeed, marriage is especially suited by its nature to the gracing effect of redemption because it is a "forshadowing of the Incarnation."[6]

---

[3] Sermon 74.

[4] 4 Sentences, d. 26, d. 5.

[5] "Christ himself, who instituted the holy sacraments . . . brings natural love to perfection," Decree of the Council of Trent, 24 session, Nov. 11, 1563, Denz. 1799.

[6] Pope Leo XIII, Arcanum Divinae Sapientiae, Feb. 10, 1880, A.S.S., 12.

Marriage Is a Means of Redemption Based on a Union of the People of God

Because a sacrament of the New Law is an action by which Christ touches man through the Church, St. Ambrose of Milan described it as a "meeting with Christ." How is marriage a meeting with Christ? A consideration of the similarity between the sacrament of the Church and the sacrament of marriage will provide an insight. Like the mystery of Christ in the Church, a presence symbolized and made actual in the breaking of the eucharistic bread, Christian marriage is a union of believers signifying and incarnating Christ. This is why marriage provides St. Paul such a dramatic means of explaining the relationship between Christ and the Church:

> The husband is the head of the wife as Christ is the head of the church, his body . . . husbands love your wives, as Christ loved the church, and gave himself up for her . . . even so husbands should love their wives as their own bodies. He who loves his wife loves himself. For no man ever hates his own flesh, but nourishes and cherishes it, as Christ does the church, because we are members of his body. "For this reason a man shall leave his father and mother and be joined to his wife, and the two shall become one." This is a great mystery, and I take it to mean Christ and the church (Eph 5:23–32).

The union of husband and wife is like the union of Christ and the Church, but as Paul brings out in the last sentence of this passage, marriage is also one form of the union between Christ and the Church.

A third-century Christian expressed the thought of Christ's presence to the marital union in these words:

> There is but one flesh, but one spirit, between husband and wife. They pray as one, worship as one; they encourage and strengthen one another. They visit God's church together; they eat the Lord's supper at each other's side. They face difficulties, endure persecution, and share consolation together. They have no secrets from each other . . . to such as these God gives his peace. Where these two are together the Lord is also present.[7]

The great nineteenth-century theologian, Matthias J. Scheeben, beautifully explained the reason that Christians believe marriage to relate to the union of Christ and the Church:

> Christian marriage . . . has a real, essential, and intrinsic reference to the mystery of Christ's union with his Church. It is rooted in this mystery and is organically connected with it, and so partakes of its nature and

---

[7] Tertullian, *Letter to His Wife.*

mysterious character. Christian marriage is not simply a symbol of this mystery or a type which lies outside it, but an image growing out of the union of Christ with the Church and pervaded by it. For it not only symbolizes the mystery but really represents it. It represents the mystery because the mystery proves active and operative in it.[8]

More recently the Fathers of the Second Vatican Council have developed the same theme:

> As God . . . made himself present to his people through a covenant of love and fidelity, so now the Savior of men and the Spouse of the Church comes into the lives of married Christians through the sacrament of matrimony. He abides with them thereafter.[9]

Marriage as a Participation in Christ's Law of Love

"This is my commandment, that you love one another as I have loved you" (Jn 15:12). Love is the Christian law; without love even faith is "nothing" (1 Cor 13:2). A marriage without love would be like a church without love — it would be a vain and empty thing. But marriage, like the Church, provides those who enter it with a magnificent opportunity to participate in Christ's love. "Married couples . . . signify and share in that very love with which Christ loved his Bride and because of which he delivered himself up on her behalf."[10]

The natural opportunity to love offered by marriage requires a total offering of oneself. It is the bride saying, "My beloved is mine and I am his . . . I held him and would not let him go" (Song 2:16 and 3:4). It is the bridegroom answering: "You have ravished my heart, my sister, my bride . . . how sweet is your love, my sister, my bride" (Song 4:9–10). It is like the *leitourgia*, the liturgy of service and sacrifice, with which St. Paul tells the Philippians they should pour out their lives for God. Nothing short of the total service-sacrifice of the spouse meets the demands of natural marital love.

The natural love liturgy of marriage is a particularly fine basis for the kind of love which Jesus urges on man. Christ takes natural love and makes it over into redemptive love. The writers of the New Testament did not use the ordinary Greek word for love, eros. This is not because eros represented an immoral thing,[11] but because as a natural form of

---

[8] *Mysteries of Christianity* (St. Louis: Herder, 1946), p. 606.
[9] *The Pastoral Constitution on the Church in the Modern World,* art. 48.
[10] *Dogmatic Constitution on the Church,* art. 41.
[11] Some of the Greeks had very beautiful ideas of eros. Plato's heavenly eros was based on a primeval memory of the once-contemplated beauty of the divine. But eros was too limited for the Christians because it was confined to those in whom the

self-giving based on the desirability of the one loved eros did not convey the meaning of the kind of love commanded by Christ. Christian love was represented by the word agapē or agapān.[12] Agapē is translated into Latin as caritas, and into English as charity. It means God's love, for the Christian believes that the love which is God has touched man through Christ. "As the Father has loved me, so have I loved you; abide in my love" (Jn 15:9). When Jesus told the Apostles to "love one another" (Jn 15:17), this was to be done with God's love which he has given to them. St. Paul described agapē as "God's love which has been poured into our hearts" (Rom 5:5). The great test of God's love in man is his willingness to love his neighbor:

> We love because he first loved us. If anyone says "I love God," and hates his brother, he is a liar; for he who does not love his brother whom he has seen, cannot love God whom he has not seen (1 Jn 4:19–20).

For the married Christian, the primary neighbor is the spouse. The real test of a married Christian's love of God is his love of wife or husband. This is why St. Paul, when he tells the husbands of Corinth to love their wives, uses the word agapē, God's love (Eph 5:25). The married Christian creates a union of one flesh which is even something more than a natural service and sacrifice — he creates a vehicle by which God's redemptive love is brought into the world. As was written by the bishops at the Second Vatican Council: "Authentic married love is caught up into divine love and . . . enriched by Christ's redeeming power."[13]

Christian Marriage as a Share in Christ's Teaching Mission to the World

Christians believe that Jesus redeemed man through his teaching as well as through his actions. St. Clement of Alexandria, about the year 190, wrote that "The Word is our Educator who heals us . . . by his counsel."[14] The Christian, in turn, is to be a teacher to others, a witness to Christ "to the ends of the earth" (Acts 1:8). There are many ways that the Christian can participate in redemptive teaching, but marriage

---

lover sees the good and the beautiful. Christ told his followers to love even their enemies.

[12] The word philia is also used in the New Testament. It represents the love of a friend for a friend — a love of deep natural affection. An example is the friendship of Jesus and Lazarus in Jn 11:3.

[13] Supra, n. 9.

[14] The Educator, Book I.

provides a most unusual opportunity for such participation in the spread of Christ's life-giving word.[15]

A Christian husband and wife, in the very unity of their one flesh, will "instruct and encourage"[16] each other in the mystery of faith. As they make moral decisions together, as they experience the Christian life together, as they develop common attitudes about life the husband and wife should find in one another a witness to Christ.

Chrildren provide another opportunity for a share in redemptive teaching. In the family the infant is set on the road to maturity. Primitive man first evolved language and art in the context of family life, and this process is repeated in the individual child. By their procreative educational activity, the parents are forming mature human beings. Christian parents will consider Christlike attitudes to be a vital part of the maturity they want their children to achieve. Such attitudes are not the negative, irrelevant, and rule-formulated religious education which children too often encounter in a classroom but the revolutionary challenge of the Sermon on the Mount. It is an attitude which will leave the child convinced that Christianity means an unstinting love of God in the neighbor.

This is the challenge verbalized for the Christian parents by the Second Vatican Council:

> It is particularly in the Christian family, enriched by the grace and the office of the sacrament of matrimony, that from the earliest years children should be taught, according to faith received in baptism, to have a knowledge of God, to worship him and to love their neighbor. . . . Let parents clearly recognize how a truly Christian family is vital for the life and development of God's own people.[17]

---

[15] In the third century the Greek Christian Father Methodius pictured the growth of the Church in words applied by Genesis to marriage: "the words 'increase and multiply' are daily fulfilled as the Church grows . . . the Church was removed from his side as a power by which all may grow strong . . . and his side is the Spirit of truth . . . by which all are conceived into eternal life" *The Symposium*, Logos 3: Thalia.

[16] *Supra*, n. 7.

[17] *Declaration on Christian Education*, art. 3.

CHAPTER 5

SEXUAL LOVE AS GOD'S
GIFT TO MAN

The Historical Failure of Some Christians to Appreciate Sex as the Gift of God

If marriage is a means of sanctification, then sex must be holy. Sexual differentiation makes marriage possible. God so willed it:

> So God created man in his own image, in the image of God he created him; male and female he created them (Gen 1:27).

But throughout the history of the Church there have always been Christians who failed to recognize this gift of God. A dualistic puritanism which sees sex as something shameful has persisted in certain parts of the Church. Paradoxically, the young Christian is today faced with a philosophy which sees sex as a plaything, a toy to be used in idle pseudo-sophisticated leisure, a foldout picture in a magazine. Both puritanism and the playboy philosophy are based on a common error — they fail to see sex as a good integrated into human life as a means of fulfilling the creative and redemptive plans of God. By holding sex apart from life, and making it an absolute evil or an absolute good for its own sake, the puritan and the playboy have perverted one of God's most beautiful gifts.

One reason that some of the early Christians had a perverted idea of sex was the popularity of neo-Platonic dualism at the very time that the Fathers of the Church were attempting to verbalize the ideals of the Gospel. The most influential Latin theologian of the third century, Tertullian, could not understand how sex could relate to the "spiritual" destiny of man.[1] The biographer of St. Martin of Tours, Sulpicius Severus, quotes him as saying that "marriage relates to indulgence" and describing marriage as a field which has not lost the beauty of the grass but does lack lovely flowers because sexual union has removed the beauty of virginity.[2] Even the great Augustine of Hippo, while attempting to defend marriage from the attacks of heretics, wrote: "detest the members of the human body as adultery is detested; indeed adultery would not exist but for these members."[3]

Although the charge that "patristic ideals . . . pronounced a curse on sex"[4] is a false generalization, many of the Fathers of the Church were unable to see sex as an element of man's religious experience. Neo-Platonic dualism and unnecessarily frantic attempts to defend the Christian ideal of virginity explain some of these failures, but incorrect knowledge of physiology also colored patristic thinking. This must be remembered by any person who wants to evaluate the thinking of the Fathers on sex fairly. For example, it was commonly thought in the fifth century that sexual relations, especially at a time when conception could not occur, were physically and mentally debilitating. This led men

---

[1] In most of his comments on sex, Tertullian conveys the impression that marriage is primarily a means of avoiding concupiscence. As he increasingly favored the teachings of the Montanists, his writings became more anti-sexual. Just before his final break with the Church his anti-sexual spiritualism became apparent: "We must renounce the things of the body in order that we can produce the fruit of the spirit. Strive to free yourself from the one to whom you must pay the marital debt . . . , you may not like this but it is in your own best interest." From the *Exhortation to Chastity*.

[2] *The Second Dialogue.*

[3] *Against Julian*, Book 5.

[4] R. Briffault, *The Mothers, the Matriarchal Theory of Social Origins* (New York: Macmillan, 1931), Vol. III, p. 506.

such as St. Leo I and St. Vincent of Lerins to believe that sexual intercourse which did not result in conception was venially sinful.[5]

During the "dark ages" (ca. A.D. 500 to 1000) the practice of Christianity was reduced to superstition in parts of Europe. When ignorance
of sex combined with religious superstition, some startling ideas about
sexual morality gained currency in the Church. Some purportedly Christian writing expressed the view that sexual pleasure is evil; a good example is found in the famous *Responsum Gregorii M. ad Augustinum
Episcopum*, a forged letter dating from about A.D. 730. Some eighth-
and ninth-century monastic documents refer to the sex organs as the
"evil members." Some local churches practiced pagan purification rites
for those who had enjoyed sexual coitus or experienced childbirth.
This extreme suspicion of sex reached its most intense point in the
Irish church of the pre-medieval period. Irish puritanism affected the
continent through the numerous missionaries sent to Europe by that
church during the dark ages. The idea that confession had to intervene
between marital coitus and communion gained great popularity in the
Irish church. Some Irish writers even expressed the weird thought that
nocturnal pollution of the male sperm and menstruation in the female
were curses.

This high tide of anti-sexualism in the Church receded during the
period, but left its mark on the thinking of some Christians. The
Church resisted the anti-sex teachings of the Albigensians[6] and the
Jansenists. Because of the aberrations which have occurred in Christian
thinking about sex, many theologians down through the century have
taken considerable pains to set forth the true Christian belief about sex.
The first great theologian of the post-Apostolic Church, St. Clement of
Alexandria, rejected the influence which the neo-Platonic dualists were
having on Christian thought; he reminded them that, in attacking the
flesh of man, they were discrediting the "flesh which the Lord himself
assumed . . . and the body which he healed for so many sick." Clement
was confident of the holiness of sex: "I know that marriage is made holy

---

[5] St. Leo manifested a conviction that the spirit must win out over matter if a
man is to reach the highest plane of the Christian life. He urged a married man
who was ordained to the priesthood to make his marriage "spiritual" and cease "carnal"
union. *Letter to Rusticus, Bishop of Norbonne.*

[6] The most famous Albigensian sect, the Cathars, only carried anti-sexual spiritualism
to its logical conclusion. They believed that childbirth was evil because it forced a
new human spirit into degrading bodily form. If the human body was evil, then it
should be destroyed; suicide was, therefore, the great Catharist sacrament.

and that the union of bodies is holy."[7] The gentle and influential Alexandrian also wrote that "it is not the terms, or the sex organs, or marital coitus, which is obscene. Neither is the knee, or the thigh, or the names we give to them or the use made of them obscene. Indeed, the sexual parts of man's body deserve not to be treated with prudery but with privacy. It is only the immoral use of sex which is obscene."[8] It was the great bishop of Constantinople, St. John Chrysostum, who coined the term "gift of God" for sex in the fourth century. In one sermon he described marital coitus as "taking of the purest gold and mingling of it with other gold." He said that those who felt shame at his words were insulting the gift of God, were blushing at that which is good. "By showing shame for marriage," he concluded, "you are condemning God who willed these things."[9]

In the medieval period the most influential Christian theologians insisted on the holiness of sex. Abelard, St. Albert the Great, Robert Courson, St. Thomas Aquinas, and especially, St. Bonaventure defended the goodness of marital coitus. The first medieval theologian to write an entire tract on marriage, Hugh of St. Victor, saw in sexual union the sacramental form by which the unity of Christ and the Church was represented.[10] To say that Christian theology ultimately triumphed over those who would separate sex from its place in God's creative plan is to say the obvious; but some consideration of that triumph has a place in a theology of marriage because the proponents of nonrealistic views of sex are always confronting the Christian.

Divine Witness to the Holiness of Sex

To the Christian Jesus is the visible sign of God to man. But the Word did not become flesh in a vacuum; he became human in the womb of a Jewish girl. The gospel story of the annunciation holds great implications for the Christian's idea of sex. It was within the power of God to achieve the Incarnation in any way; the Word could have become flesh through a human union of Joseph and Mary. But God chose a way which demonstrates the dignity of sex more fully than any other event

---

[7] Against Jovinian.

[8] "Against Obscenity," in The Educator, Book II.

[9] Sermon 12 on the Epistle to the Colossians.

[10] For a brief summary of Hugh's ideas, see E. Schillebeeckx, Marriage, Human Reality and Saving Mystery, Vol. II, cited in the bibliography, pp. 320–324.

in human history. In St. Luke's Gospel the promise is given to Mary: "The Holy Spirit will come upon you and the power of the Most High will overshadow you; therefore the child to be born will be called holy, the Son of God" (Lk 1:35). Luke then goes on to relate how Mary described these happenings to her cousin Elizabeth:

> My soul magnifies the Lord,
> and my spirit rejoices in God, my savior,
> for he has regarded the low estate of his handmaiden.
> For behold, henceforth all generations
> will call me blessed;
> for he who is mighty has done great things for me.
>
>   (Lk 1:46–49)

It is apparent that in these passages Luke is recording the belief of the primitive Church that God intervened directly among men and united divine power to the human sexuality of Mary to generate Jesus in human flesh. To express this momentous happening, the Nicene Creed used these words: "he came down from heaven and was made flesh by the Holy Spirit in the Virgin Mary."[11]

Theologians describe the Incarnation as a work "ad extra," i.e., a work of the Trinity outside of the relations existing between the divine persons. God has used his divine power directly to cause the Incarnation in the womb of Mary. No more beautiful witness to the holiness of sex could be found than a direct use of it by God himself to bring about the central event in human history.

Sexual Love Is a Vocation to a Personal Union of Sharing

Christians speak of marriage as a vocation, a calling from God to lead a particular way of life. It is a calling to carry out a life of creation and redemption by the human power of marital love. This power of love is based in sex. But the modern world strives to convince us that sex is a fleeting moment. Some writers, even theologians, describe sex as a passion to be discharged. But human sex is something more than a passing contact, something more than a passion. It involves moments of ecstatic contact, it does bring a physical peace, but more importantly

---

[11] Other creeds express the same thought in even clearer words: "the Virgin did not have intercourse with man but was made fruitful by the Holy Spirit," Creed of Toledo (A.D. 625), Denz. 533. "Not with human seed but by the Holy Spirit did she conceive the divine Word," Lateran Council (A.D. 649), Denz. 503 "Jesus was conceived of the Holy Spirit . . . in the womb of the Virgin Mary," Pope Paul IV, Cum Quorundam (A.D. 1555), Denz. 1880.

human sex is open to development as a wonderfully complex but effective means of communion between lovers.

This phrase "indulge in sexual intercourse" says nothing to married lovers because to them sex is not an indulgence; it is a deeply personal relationship between two human beings. Through sex, husband and wife affirm and express the love they have built and are building. Marital sexual intimacy of any kind relates to the union of communion existing between the lovers.

Human sexual response and activity are not easily perfected. Sex doesn't just happen to human beings. Many young married couples are misled on this because they have failed to realize sex as a part of their vocation. They know that one must strive to build his vocation; in marriage, they know that one doesn't easily become a good homemaker, an expert in consumer economics, and a good parent. But they somehow do not understand that sex as a part of marital relation must be similarly built together. In every respect successful marriage requires a lifetime of dedicated building, and this is as true of sex as it is of everything else.

When a man and woman realize that sex is God's gift for them to build and develop, then they can start to overcome their personal inadequacies as lovers and grow up together in the use of this gift. The fathers of the Second Vatican Council expressed power for growth embodied in sexual love:

> The biblical Word of God several times urges . . . the married to nourish and develop their wedlock by pure conjugal love and undivided affection . . . this love is eminently human . . . it can enrich the expressions of body and mind with a unique dignity, ennobling these expressions as special ingredients and signs of the friendship distinctive of marriage.[12]

---

[12] *The Pastoral Constitution on the Church in the Modern World*, art. 49.

CHAPTER 6

THE PURPOSE OF MARRIAGE

A theological discussion of the purposes of marriage does not center on the goals which motivate individual persons to marry. The Catechism composed at the Council of Trent suggests that there are many good subjective reasons for people to marry; companionship, desire for family life, need for an heir, wealth, beauty, etc.[1] Probably the great majority of brides and grooms would not be able to state clearly the reasons which motivate them to marry.

Purpose, as distinguished from subjective goals, means the ends which the Creator means to achieve through the marital state. To answer the question "what is the purpose of marriage?" one must examine the goods which marriage does, or should, produce in human life.

Many different answers are given to the question by contemporary

---

[1] See J. A. McHugh and C. J. Callan, *Catechism of the Council of Trent* (New York: Joseph Wagner, Inc., 1937), Part II, Chap. 8, p. 343.

Catholic writers. But differences among Catholics on this question are not new. In the nineteenth century German theologians such as Linsenmann, Probst, and Koch debated the problem. Differences among theologians led the Holy Office to forbid Catholic writers publicly to "deny that the principal end of marriage is the procreation and education of children and to say that the secondary ends of marriage are not subordinated to the principal end, but that all ends are absolutely equal and independent of one another."[2] This cooled the atmosphere for debate of the question for a few years, but in the late fifties and early sixties of this century a variety of opinions once again began to appear in Catholic writing.

It must be understood that, in making the following breakdown of opinions, the author is generalizing. Space does not permit an analysis of the writings of even a few theologians on the subject. Since we are generalizing, it would be unfair to attribute the opinions outlined to any specific author. The opinions are presented only to indicate trends of thinking in Catholic circles today.

One Solution: The Primary Purpose of Marriage Is the Procreation of Children

This solution has two variants. One group of theologians described the procreation of children as the primary purpose of marriage from the nature of sexual love. Sexual love expression, which distinguishes marital love from other forms of self-giving, reaches its consummation in coitus. In sexual intercourse the whole tendency of the couple's interaction on each other, at least physically, is to move the sperm into the body of the woman where an egg might be awaiting fertilization. Conception, they conclude, is the natural end or goal of coitus, the most sublime expression of marital love. Most modern theologians reject this approach, holding that it reduces marriage to a mechanical institution interpreted only in a biological framework.

Among those who reject the biological approach to the purpose of marriage, there are many theologians (probably the majority) who conclude that the primary purpose of marriage is the procreation of children, but do so for very different reasons. Marriage is the most fundamental of social institutions, the basis of society and civilization. From the viewpoint of the human commonweal the most significant

---

[2] Decree of March 1, 1944.

purpose of the family is to produce and educate the citizen of the future to maturity. On the success of the family's educational work depends the ultimate good of every human society: the race, the state, the local community, and the Church. From society's point of view, the primary goal of marriage is the procreation of children; procreation here means much more than physical conception.

In this scheme the mutual companionship or fulfillment found by man and wife in marriage is only a secondary purpose of marriage. This is not to say that it is secondary to the couple, only that it is a less significant goal of marriage from the viewpoint of human society. This view looks at marriage in its function as "the beginning and basis of human society."[3] Since law is society-oriented, it is not surprising that the Canon Law of the Church adopts this theory: "the primary end of marriage is the procreation and education of children" (Canon 1013).

A common criticism of this solution is that it separates two things which in the reality of marriage are inseparable. It is the mutual fulfill-ment of husband and wife which makes them fully effective participants in familial, procreative work.

Another Solution: The Primary Purpose of Marriage Is the Conjugal Love of Husband and Wife

Influenced by the New Testament exegesis and the primacy of charity in contemporary moral thought, many Catholics now advocate that the primary purpose of marriage be described as conjugal love. They describe marriage as a "mandate of life focused primarily on leading one life together in conjugal love and secondarily on building a good family life together."[4] This viewpoint has a great existential appeal because it gives preferences to the realities of marital life as husband and wife experience them. A person enters marriage because he wants to build a life of marital love with this other person; the goods of family life merely flow from this personal commitment to the other.

The real difficulty with this solution is that it retains a primary-secondary approach to the purposes of marriage; today more and more writers are asking if such a preferential ranking of the purposes of marriage is needed.

---

[3] *Decree on the Apostolate of the Laity*, art. 11.
[4] Bishop William M. Beekers, television address to the Catholics of Netherlands, April, 1963. From newspaper reports.

Another Solution: Speak of the Purposes of Marriage as Integrated Goods

There can be no doubt that a division of the purposes of marriage into primary and secondary categories is frequently confusing to many Catholics. The theologian may understand that a primary purpose is such only from the viewpoint of society, but at the pastoral level understanding of this approach is usually at a minimum. Pope Pius XI described marriage as "the blending of life as a whole and the mutual interchange and exchange thereof,"[5] and there is a growing feeling in the theological community that statements on the purpose of marriage should reflect this integration of life values.

St. Augustine described the goods achieved by marriage as "offspring, fidelity, sacrament."[6] This was adopted by Aquinas who explained it in terms of human nature:

> The first end, offspring, is found in marriage because man is an animal; the second end, fidelity in common life together, is found in marriage because man is human; the third end, sacrament, is found in marriage because man is a Christian.[7]

There are some writers who would like to return to the Augustinian-Thomistic three-goods of marriage statement, but with a treatment of these as integrated ends. When people marry, they commit themselves to a human community based on conjugal love; this community is open to the procreation of offspring and to the growth of the "new creature" (2 Cor 5:17) in Christ. Thus marriage has a triple blessing of love, children and sacrament.

The Author's Opinion

The author shares the dissatisfaction which many theologians feel for the solutions based on a primary-secondary distinction among the purposes of marriage. He finds it interesting that in the statement on marriage in the *Pastoral Constitution on the Church in the Modern World*, the bishops insisted that "matrimony . . . and conjugal love are ordained for the procreation and education of children and find in

---

[5] *Casti Connubii*, A.A.S., 22 (1930).
[6] *On the Advantage of Marriage*.
[7] *Summa of Theology*, Suppl., Q. 65, art. 1.

them their ultimate crown,"[8] but avoided any primary-secondary distinction in speaking of the "various benefits and purposes"[9] of marriage. In speaking of the procreation of children, the bishops described husband and wife as "glorifying the Creator and striving toward fulfillment in Christ."[10] This would seem an ideal way of describing the purpose of marriage itself.

Marriage exists in order to give man a share in creation and redemption. A man and woman marry in order to give themselves totally in love to each other. This love leads them into a relationship of service-sacrifice which enables them to participate ever more fully in the mystery of creation. They ever more deeply procreate the loving life of one flesh which exists between them; should they conceive or adopt children, the educational tasks of each day become a procreative challenge. To the extent that the Christian couple make their marriage a "domestic church,"[11] they are sharing in redemption. Some may argue that such a general statement of the purpose of marriage has little value; this author believes it has great value because it requires married Christians to consider seriously and responsibly how they can make their marriages ever more effective instruments of creation and redemption.

A SELECT BIBLIOGRAPHY FOR PART I

An asterisk (*) indicates works available in paperback editions.

Bier, W. (ed.), Marriage: A Psychological and Moral Approach (New York: Fordham University Press, 1965).

Bowman, H., A Christian Interpretation of Marriage (Philadelphia: Westminster Press, 1959).

Brav, S., Marriage and the Jewish Tradition (New York: Philosophical Library, 1951).

*Caffarel, H. (ed.), Marriage Is Holy (Notre Dame: Fides, 1957).

Cervantes, Lucius, And God Made Man and Woman (Chicago: Henry Regnery, 1959).

Cunningham, L.; Donlan, T.; Rock, A., Toward Marriage In Christ (Dubuque: Priory Press, 1962).

*Daniel-Rops, H., et al., Love is Forever (Chicago: Scepter Books, 1964).

Dantec, F., Love is Life (Notre Dame: University of Notre Dame Press, 1963).

DeFabregues, J., Christian Marriage (New York: Hawthorn Books, 1959).

*DeSmedt, E., Married Love (Notre Dame: Fides, 1965).

Ford, J. and Kelly, G., Contemporary Moral Theology, Vol. II: Marriage Questions (Westminster: Newman, 1963).

---

[8] Art. 48.   [10] Art. 49.
[9] Ibid.   [11] Dogmatic Constitution on the Church, art. 11.

Gosling, J., *Marriage and the Love of God* (New York: Sheed and Ward, 1965).

Grelot, P., *Man and Wife in Scripture* (New York: Herder and Herder, 1964).

Guitton, J., *Essay on Human Love* (London: Rockcliff, 1951).

Häring, B., *Marriage in the Modern World* (Westminster: Newman Press, 1966).

Kerns, J., *The Theology of Marriage: The Historical Development of Christian Attitudes Toward Sex and Sanctity in Marriage* (New York: Sheed and Ward, 1964).

Leclercq, J., *Marriage, A Great Sacrament* (New York: Macmillan, 1957).

McDonagh, E. (ed.), *The Meaning of Christian Marriage* (New York: Alba House, 1963).

Messenger, E., *Two in One Flesh* (Westminster: Newman Press, 1955).

Oraison, M., *The Human Mystery of Sexuality* (New York: Sheed and Ward, 1967).

*——— *Man and Wife* (New York: Macmillan, 1962). (Originally published under title *Union in Marital Love*, 1958).

Pius XII, Pope, *Dear Newlyweds* (New York: Farrar, Straus, and Cudahy, 1961).

Planque, D., *The Christian Couple* (Notre Dame: Fides, 1963).

*——— *The Theology of Sex in Marriage* (Notre Dame: Fides, 1962).

*Schillebeeckx, E., *Marriage: Human Reality and Saving Mystery* (New York: Sheed and Ward, 1965):

Vol. I: *Marriage in the Old Testament.*

Vol. II: *Marriage in the History of the Church.*

(In hardback edition both volumes are in one binding).

Shideler, M., *The Theology of Romantic Love* (New York: Harper and Bros., 1962).

*Thibon, G., *What God Has Joined Together* (Chicago: Henry Regnery, 1952).

*Trevett, R., *The Church and Sex* (New York: Hawthorn Books, 1964).

*——— *The Tree of Life* (New York: J. P. Kenedy, 1963).

von Hildebrand, D., *In Defense of Purity* (Baltimore: Helicon Press, 1962).

*——— *Marriage* (New York: Longmans, Green and Co., 1959).

von Hornstein, F. X. and Faller, A., *Sex-Love-Marriage* (New York: Herder and Herder, 1964).

The reader will find that the following periodicals, while not professional theological journals, frequently contain popular articles relevant to this part:

ACT, Voice of the C.F.M.
America
Ave Maria
Commonweal
Jubilee
Marriage
National Catholic Reporter
Report

PART II

PREPARING FOR CHRISTIAN MARRIAGE

CHAPTER 7

EARLY PREPARATION:
A CHRISTIAN SEX EDUCATION

Educating the Child to See Sex as the Vehicle of Love

Christians believe that marriage is a vocation of love. "Through their faithful love married people will become witnesses of the mystery of that love which the Lord revealed to the world."[1]

Marital love is distinguished from other forms of love by the fact of complementary sexual differentiation between the lovers. A man cannot appreciate the design of the Creator for marital love if he has a perverted idea of the power of sexual love which God has implanted in human beings. Adults who are charged with the responsibility of educating children are grossly negligent if they fail to help the child achieve a Christian vision of sex. The fathers of the Second Vatican Council have described this responsibility:

---

[1] *Pastoral Constitution on the Church in the Modern World*, art. 52.

A true education aims at the formation of the human person with respect to his ultimate goal, and simultaneously with respect to the good of those societies of which, as a man, he is a member, and in whose responsibilities, as an adult, he will share. As a consequence, with the help of advances in psychology and in the art and science of teaching, children and young people should be assisted in the harmonious development of their physical, moral and intellectual endowments . . . they should be helped to acquire gradually a more mature sense of responsibility toward ennobling their own lives through constant effort, and toward pursuing authentic freedom. As they advance in years, they should be given positive and prudent sexual education.[2]

A Christian sex education must include two elements: a gradual communication of information about the functional aspects of male and female sexuality, and the progressive development of an awe-filled respect for this loving power with which the Creator has endowed man. Parents and educators must give a child more than a technical knowledge of sex. The attitude of adult toward sex is largely the result of his childhood experience and education. Seen in this perspective, sex education becomes a step laden with tremendous implications for the future life of marital love which the child may some day choose to live.

The Roles of the Home, the School, and the Church in Sex Education

The parents alone are the educators of children in the fullest sense. They are the one constant and ever-present educational factor in the life of the child from birth to adulthood. The child is completely dependent on them in the developmentally vital first few years of life. They alone observe and aid the unfolding of the child's concerns, interests, and needs day after day, year after year. It is to the parents that the child naturally turns to answer its questions, guide its actions, heal its hurts. The Second Vatican Council stressed this in the *Decree on Education*:

> Hence, parents must be acknowledged as the first and foremost educators of their children. Their role as educators is so decisive that scarcely anything can compensate for their failure in it.[3]

The home is the most fundamental of all educational institutions, and it is there that sex education should primarily be given.

The parents are the only ones in a position to oversee the continuing sex education of their children; they are also in the best position to help

---

[2] *The Declaration on Christian Education*, art. 1.
[3] *Ibid.*, art. 3.

the child see sex in the perspective of love. Christians believe that sex is not solitary but social in nature. Within a happy home, in a family in which love is a daily reality, sex education becomes something much more than mere instruction in physical hygiene. It becomes part of the process of recognizing the God who is love reflected in his creation. "For by the greatness of the beauty, and of the creature, the creator of them may be seen, so as to be known thereby" (Wis 13:5).

This is not to say that the school and the Church can play no role in sex education. The school can help the adolescent or teen-ager correct the many, mistaken notions of sex which arise from children's rumors and stories; it can give the child a more advanced technical knowledge of sex in biology and hygiene programs and can help the parents develop Christian attitudes in the children by reinforcing fundamental moral ideas about sex. But the school and the Church can succeed in these tasks only if the parents have done the basic job. The six-year-old entering school, the adolescent in the pew of the Church, the teen-ager sitting in the secondary school biology class — these already have developed basic life-outlooks on sex largely due to what they learned in the home. Until the parents have answered the basic questions and pointed the child toward a truly Christian conception of sex the Church and the school will be able to accomplish very little in the task of sex education.

The Impropriety of Negative-Repressive Attitudes in Sex Education

All education should be positive. A sex education which leaves a child only with a set of prohibitions, with no understanding of God's design as it is found in functional aspects of sex, with a feeling that sex is an evil part of life and must be repressed — this is not a Christian sex education. The sex education of the Christian child must be directed toward the development of the virtue of chastity, the virtue by which man uses sex in accord with the plan of the Creator.

> Especially in the heart of their own families, young people should be aptly and seasonably instructed about the dignity, duty, and expression of married love. Trained thus in the cultivation of chastity, they will be able at a suitable age to enter a marriage of their own after an honorable courtship.[4]

A negative-repressive sex education falls far short of the high ideal for sex education which the Council Fathers expressed.

---

[4] *The Pastoral Constitution on the Church in the Modern World*, art. 49.

A child is naturally curious about everything it experiences and longs to know the "what" and "why" of its own person. This wholesome desire can be thwarted by a parent who discourages the child from asking about sex, and what was natural curiosity can be replaced by a morbid interest in bodily functions. Still worse, if the parents convey a purely negative and totally repressive idea of sex, the sensitive child will begin to think that God's act of creating man male and female must be tinged with evil. That such a perversion of the idea of God and his creation can occur because of a faulty idea of sex should be apparent from the repetition of spiritualist-dualist heresies in every century of Church history.

Catholic college students have frequently complained to this author about the constant emphasis on sexual sins in their retreats and moral theology courses. Yet many of these same students will say "nobody ever really talks to us about sex." These expressions are not contradictory. Dialogue with these students revealed that many adults, i.e., parents, teachers, and pastors, had given them limited information and abundant negative prohibitions about sex, but no one had ever taken the time to help them understand how sex relates to, and functions in, a community of human love. They have been told over and over "Don't masturbate," "Don't pet," "Don't steady date," "Don't get pregnant." But, that sex is an integral part of the Creator's plan for man's achieving of holiness, that it is a means of bringing redemptive love into the world, that it is the natural power which enables a man to perform one of the seven supernatural acts of Christ in his church: all of this they were not told.

This is the essential error of a purely negative-repressive approach to sex education; it gives the child only a set of prohibitory rules instead of a Christian vision of sex. It gives him stones instead of bread. Many of the books written to aid parents in the work of sex education only encourage this negative-repressive approach. They are filled with supposed guidelines for young people which can be summed up this way: when it comes to sex develop a lot of hobbies, pray hard, and take good cold showers!

A Positive Approach to Sex Education

Sex education which leads the child to view sex as a part of the creative-redemptive plans for the universe must be based on the premise that the child can integrate his knowledge of sex into his total educational experience at a given age. A positive program of sex education is difficult to achieve because, like any education, it cannot be accomplished in a half-dozen parent-child talks about the facts of life. It requires years of attention and response to the needs of the individual child. It is a day-after-day, year-after-year work. But the end result of a positive sex education will be something more than a robot filled only with prohibitory notions of sex or a rebellious college student who finds traditional "social conventions about sex" repulsive to his reason. A positive sex education, involving years of devoted effort by Christian parents, can produce a human being who is capable of using sex as a vehicle of love. Such a human being would be well worth the labor required of the parent-educators.

The late Fritz Tillmann, in whose debt so many contemporary moral theologians stand, liked to stress the danger which prudish and mistaken ideas about sex can hold for a child's outlook on life. The Christian, by his vocation, is sworn to upholding the goodness and beauty of God-given life: "O, Lord, how manifold are thy works! In thy wisdom thou made them all, the earth is full of thy creatures — may the glory of the Lord endure forever, may the Lord rejoice in his works" (Ps 104:24, 31). The Christian belief that life is a gift of God which must be respected and appreciated in every human act should be encouraged in the child. The child sees many forms of life around him, and he must be shown that these "praise the name of the Lord" (Ps 148:5). By word and example, the youngster can be led to see the beauty of a flower, the affection of a dog, the sound of a baby attempting to form words — and from all of these he can develop a thrilling sense of what it means to be a creature of God. "For thou didst form my inward parts, thou didst knit me together in my mother's womb" (Ps 139, 14).

The child whose sense of awe-filled love of God's creation is highly developed can only respect himself, his body, his emotions. He will realize that being a boy or a girl is not something shameful but an exciting and wonderful aspect of God's creative act. He must be encouraged to touch different fabrics, see different colors, smell different odors. His parents can show him how to love life rather than spoil it. When such a child becomes a man, the beauty he sees in a girl will not be an object to conquer but a quality in another human being whom he can love. When such a child becomes a woman, the strength she finds in a man will not be a social meal ticket but a beautiful attribute of the one she loves. The young man or woman who reverence what God has made them, and respect the power of sexual love he gave them, should be the result of a positive sex education.

A Positive Sex Education Requires a Direct and Honest Approach

Any form of true education must be built around the needs of the child. This is true of sex education. The atmosphere in the home must be conducive to an honest and forthright meeting of the child's needs. A child begins to learn about his body very early, and this need for self-discovery must not be discouraged by the parents. The infant of a few months will examine his hands, then its legs and toes. As part of this self-discovery, the child of about a year or a year and a half will often finger his genitals or even display these proudly for the parents. The parents should react no differently to this than they did to interest the child previously showed in his toes.

The toilet-training stage is an important part of a young child's experience of growing up. Some parents, anxious to eliminate the inconveniences of diapers, try to force bowel training on the child before he is ready for it. This violates a cardinal rule of education: the good of the child takes precedence over the convenience of the teacher. During the second year of life most children learn in a limited way that they can control bowel or bladder movements. If the child has been given a potty-seat in which he is allowed (not forced) to sit, the stage has been set for the learning of a very important principle — the human being has some kind of control over his body. The actual development of this control is produced by a combination of factors, among which are a desire to please the parents, the desire to imitate the bathroom practices of the parents, pride in the accomplishment of having created something with his body. Many unprepared parents miss the significance of this last mentioned factor. They confuse the child by reproaching him if he attempts to touch a bowel movement or by immediately taking the bowl of urine and flushing it away. The puritanical notion that cleanliness is next to godliness must not cause an anxious parent to force the child into quickly disposing of "dirt." A passion for cleanliness is fine, but it is clearly subordinate to the need of the child to discover that bodily functions and control are a natural part of human life. It is not likely that a child who sees his parents taking bodily functions in stride will develop a morbid interest therein. The contrary is true. Most children will master toilet training between the ages of 18 and 36 months. The significant thing is not the age of the child, but the attitude with which he emerges from the experience. If the parents have conveyed a sense of bodily shame to the child, they will find the subsequent work of sex education that much more difficult.

When the child learns to talk, he will start to ask his parents questions about many things. Many pediatricians caution parents to expect the first questions about sex between the ages of two and a half and three and a half. The child usually begins his inquiry right where the Bible begins its description of the human race: "Male and female — he created them" (Gen 1:27). The parents may not recognize that the child is asking about male-female differences because of the form in which the question is asked. Certainly, the child doesn't realize that he is asking a question about sex. Most frequently, the question why are boys and girls different is brought on by some fear. A little girl may feel that she is sick or inadequate because she doesn't have a penis like a brother or neighbor boy; a little boy may fear that his penis will break off because he saw a little girl without one. All authorities agree that, if the parents treat questions about this lightly or become angry, the anxiety of the child will only increase and considerable confusion about the differences between male and female will result in the child's thinking. The child's fears should be diminished by identifying him or her with the parent of the same sex. If the little girl can be led to appreciate that her mother, like her, doesn't have a penis and that this is normal and natural, her subsequent questions about the processes of conception and birth can be answered much more satisfactorily. The same is true of the little boy who realizes that he and his father are very much alike.

Sometimes around three and a half to four and a half, most children begin to ask questions which are more explicitly about sexual functions. The importance of the parents' answers to these questions cannot be minimized. These questions indicate a real need on the part of the child, a need which must be fulfilled here and now. The question may appear silly to the parents, but no question that a young child asks is silly from his viewpoint. If the question is not answered, the sense of rapport which parent and child should be building during these years will decline and the child will soon learn to look elsewhere for its knowledge of life. Many parents who complain that they do not understand the adolescent, or that their teen-agers do not talk to them, have only themselves to blame. That child was once very young and totally dependent on them. If when that child asked their help in understanding life the parents ignored him, or were dishonest with him, the parent-child relationship began to break down at that point.

Five principles should guide parents in answering their children's questions. *First, every answer given should be honest.* Fables or lies can only do harm both to the child and the parent-child relationship. *Second, only the question which is asked should be answered.* Parents can easily fall into the trap which a good teacher will avoid, i.e., the tendency to use the occasion of a child's question to tell him several other things he did not ask about. This is very dangerous, when speaking to a young child about sex, because his question represents a specific, individual need. Going beyond the question will only confuse him and create new problems before he has solved old ones. The question must always be answered from the child's point of view. What he needs to know is the critical consideration, not what the parents feel he should know. This will not be true when the child starts to approach puberty, but it is fundamental to early sex education. A good example is found in one of the first questions children ask: "where do babies come from?" If he is told they "come from mommy and daddy puts them there" he has been told too much. A child of four is not normally prepared to cope with ideas about the father's role in having babies. The father may be a playmate, but to a child the mother is obviously the important worker when it comes to babies. The child should be told simply that babies come from their mothers, without adding any confusing information which will distract the child from his naturally developing curiosity. When the child has had time to consider this answer, he will then ask further questions about why and how babies are inside the mother. Again, the need to meet the particular concern of the child is apparent. Emphasizing the protective bag inside the mother in which the baby grows until it is big enough to live outside will help answer the child's need.

Third, questions should be answered in simple and understandable language. Many parents attempt to answer their children's questions with scientific or semi-scientific language. In describing where the baby is located inside the mother, they will use the terms uterus or womb. The problem with such terms is that they are not descriptive. Most authorities urge that children should be taught about sexual functions in picturesque language. The proper technical terms can be taught after the child has developed a picture of the process about which he has asked. An example is found in another question which most children ask. Some variant of "how do babies come out of the mother" is frequently asked once the child has digested the idea of the baby being in the mother. Telling him that the baby passes through the vagina is no way to describe the process of birth to a four-year-old. "When the baby is able to breathe and put food in its mouth, it wants to come out and it then leaves mommy through a hole in her body" is a much more effective answer. If the attitudes which the child developed during toilet training were normal and healthy, he will know that holes in the body are good and necessary to life functions.

Further questions about birth will follow. The naturalness of the birth passage should be stressed. A child, particularly a girl, can be psychologically scarred because her mother presented birth as a painful experience before the child was able to cope with pain. To a child, pain is totally evil; that good can be associated with pain can be appreciated only by a sophisticated and mature human being. It is not dishonest to stress the naturalness of childbirth rather than pain. To the contrary, it is following the second principle discussed above. The child wants to know how the baby comes out, not the mother's experience in birth. The good of the child is paramount, and to achieve that good the child's questions, not the parent's difficulties, must be answered.

Fourth, a question must be answered consistently as many times as it is asked. When a child receives an answer to a question about sex, he will usually ponder it and then ask the same question again. And again. The child is not necessarily showing dissatisfaction with the answer; he is only trying to understand something which appears to him as both beautiful and complex. He wants to be sure that his picture is accurate. Any impatience with this repetition will erode the child's confidence in the parents. Good teachers know that recapitulation is essential to the art of education; parents must learn this art in dealing with their children. Frequently, the child will ask a question of his parents separately and then together. The parents must cooperate to see that the child is receiving answers which are both honest and consistent.

Fifth, the answers given to the child must convey a sense of familial privacy about sex. The child should be encouraged to speak his mind about sex within the family, but the parents must subtly suggest that these things should not be discussed with playmates. This should be done with care not to convey a feeling that it is shameful to speak of sex. The emphasis is to be on modesty. The child must be convinced that sex is not a casual matter but a very important human power. This power should be related to a very special community, the family, and it is best discussed within the personal relationships of family life.

If a sense of rapport has been built up between parents and child, these questions will continue to be asked into the immediate pre-school and early school years. The exact questions will be largely formed by the child's own experience. If the mother is pregnant, this will produce a flood of questions. Allowing a five or six-year-old to feel the baby moving inside mother can only increase his reverence for the mystery of life. Animal observation is an additional source of questions, but some people put too much stress on this. Unless observation of animal mating and birth is accompanied by a well-rounded sex education, the child will develop a very mechanical idea of sex. But animal observation as a part of sex education can show a child the naturalness of sex. Such a child is not likely to confuse the artificial TV version with the real thing.

In time the child will begin to ask questions about the father. In the first years of a child's life the father is often a mysterious figure. He may be a wonderful playmate and occasional worker, but in the eyes of the four-year-old, the mother is the most industrious and hard-working parent. The support function of the father will probably remain a mystery well into the teen years. When a child does begin to inquire about the father, it is frequently in connection with things he has already related to the mother. When he asks about the relationship of the father to the baby, he should then be told that "daddy puts the baby into mother." From this, the child will begin to appreciate that sex is not solitary but communal. Putting a baby into mother is one of the many good acts of love which daddy does for mommy. Presenting the father in his generative function has a tremendous advantage for the collateral, religious education of the child. Jesus taught man to think of God as his Father. The religious education of a child should begin with a vision of a loving God who is the source of all life. As the child reflects on the mystery of creation, his concomitant appreciation of his own father as the source of familial life can only deepen his understanding of the God he calls Father.

When the child enters school, he will begin to pick up mistaken ideas about sex from his companions. This is particularly true of the eight, nine, and ten-year-old. If the child has developed a sense of confidence in his parents, he will continue to ask them questions. Improper ideas should be expressly denied, but reasons should always be given. The emphasis should be on sex as a dimension of love between father and mother. It is because father loves mother that he puts a part of his body into hers and leaves a pool of seeds there. So great is this expression of love that these seeds, in the creator's plan, can join to a little egg in the mother and form a baby. If the child in fifth or sixth grade is given such a picture of love between a man and woman, he will be better prepared for the experience of puberty and will not enter the teen years with the silly ideas about sexual intercourse which even many college students have. Puberty should not be a nightmare of confusion for a child, but a time when he knows that he is growing in the development of a tremendous power of human love.

The term puberty indicates the passage from childhood to adulthood. This is difficult for Americans to appreciate because our complex technological society requires the extension of educational development well past the age of puberty. There is no set age when puberty will occur, and there are many factors which affect it. Climate is a factor, puberty usually being achieved earlier in tropical areas. Individual body characteristics may influence it, since small heavy-set children are more likely to achieve puberty before other children. Heredity may even be a factor in determining the age at which a given child will reach puberty.

Puberty in the boy is usually achieved somewhere between the ages of twelve and sixteen, although there are exceptions. The first sign of puberty is normally the growth of hair in the area of the genitals. This will be followed, frequently within a few months, by a nocturnal or seminal emission. The boy will wake to find the bed sheets wet with a sticky grey substance. The power of producing spermatozoa is the essence of puberty. But circumstantial changes in body appearance will continue for several years. Hair will grow in the armpits, the chin, and perhaps on the chest. A deepening of voice, an increase in the size of the larynx, an enlarging of the shoulders due to bone growth, change in skin texture, and a fairly intensive growth in height also occur. These remarkable changes inevitably give rise to some psychological stress. Physically, the boy has approached manhood, yet it will be years before he will be allowed the privileges and responsibilities of the adult. He will feel awkward because he has not yet become used to these changes. He will be sensitive and easily hurt.

The boy must be prepared for the great experience of puberty. If father and son have established a real sense of personal communication, this task will not be too difficult. When the boy is about ten or eleven, the father should begin to stress the need for cleanliness in the genital area. The father should show the boy how to wash the scrotum and penis. The father can easily direct this into a discussion of the changes which will come over the boy. The changes should be related to what the boy already knows about sexual love and reproduction. The boy should be encouraged to talk over problems of puberty with the father as they occur. Many young boys accidentally discover during puberty that they can draw out the seed by manipulation of the penis. If a boy has confidence in his father, he will ask about this. This can be a wonderful opportunity for a discussion of sex as an outward power of love for another human being rather than a self-seeking experience. While frankly discouraging masturbation, the father must not frighten the boy with false scare stories about physical harm in the habit. Christian education, including sex education, should never be put on a false basis. The emphasis should be on the moral use of sex based on the Creator's plan that manhood is the power which will enable the boy to give himself to the woman he will someday love. The parent who stands at his boy's side, helping him to understand the process of becoming a man, can be sure that he is fulfilling his sacramental vocation to open his child's mind to the meaning of creation and redemption.

On the average, puberty in girls occurs earlier than in boys, usually between the ages of ten and fourteen. In essence, female puberty is the discharge of an egg or ovum from the ovary.[5] Just as the production of sperm in the male is not apparent until a nocturnal emission, so ovulation is not manifested in the girl until menstruation. However, circumstantial changes in bodily appearance may precede menstruation. Growth of hair in the genital region frequently occurs before the first menstruation. Other changes, such as growth of armpit hair, growth of fat on the hips and enlargement of the pelvis, and development of the breasts may begin before or after menstruation.

The first menstruation can be a frightening experience if the girl is not prepared for it. She should be told ahead of time that menstruation is not bleeding and does not indicate sickness. Stress should be placed on the fact that menstruation is only the natural aftereffect of ovula-

---

[5] Menstruation begins sometimes before the first ovulation. Thus a girl will still be sterile for a time after puberty has begun. Some authorities prefer to apply the term *female puberty* to menstruation and the bodily changes which accompany it, reserving the word *nubility* to indicate that stage of puberty when the girl becomes fertile.

tion, that is, the production of an egg which can develop into a child in a loving embrace with her future husband. Ovulation is accompanied by the development of a protective lining in the womb wherein a child can grow and develop. But if no child is conceived, then this lining becomes unnecessary and simply passes from the body during menstruation. A mother will have many occasions to prepare a girl for these changes, and should do so several times. Many nine- or ten-year-old girls are interested in their mothers' clothing and will ask about the pads which mother wears every so often. Questions such as this should not be allowed to pass unused for preparing the girl for puberty. The mother should use the confidence which the girl has in her to stress both cleanliness and an understanding of the process by which a child becomes a woman. She must be careful not to use terms such as woman's curse or monthly illness in describing menstruation. The stress should be on the naturalness of the process as a vital part of being a woman who is capable of loving a man and bearing a child.

During puberty a girl frequently needs reassurance. The father is important here, because most girls will ask him over and over about their appearance. He must encourage her in order that she may realize that these bodily changes are not harming her, but making her into a beautiful young woman. She must be encouraged to seek advice from the mother about a feeling of heaviness or depression which might accompany menstruation. The channels of communication between parents and daughter must remain open during puberty for the girl cannot fathom the mystery of becoming a woman on her own. Continuing concern for the needs of the child is always the hallmark of a parent who takes his God-given responsibilities seriously.

This concern, manifested by an ever maturing dialogue between parent and child, must continue into the post-puberty years. The responsibilities and freedom given to the young adult will increase during the secondary school years. During these years young men and women develop reading habits in which the parents should take an interest. Actually, the parents will be largely responsible for the reading habits of the teen-ager. Their influence will have been more direct in the pre-school and early school years. But the kind of reading which teen-agers do is often subconsciously patterned after that of their parents. If the reading of the parents is largely confined to vapid women's magazines and the daily newspaper, the teen's reading habits are likely to remain at a similarly superficial level.

Reading is an important factor in the continuing sex education of the teenager, if for no other reason than the volume of published material available on sex today. The parents who have done a thorough job of sex education will not attempt to cut material on sex out of the reading diet of the teen-ager. But they will be sure that both literary and factual reading materials which reflect a Christian idea of sex are available in the home. This doesn't mean the "wholesome" entertainments which some publishers and movie makers try to pawn off as suitable for mamilies. It means reading material which complements the needs and maturity of the given child. Of course, the fact that the law in a multivalue society does not judge material obscene (i.e., as dealing "with sex in a manner speaking to purient interest," *Roth* v. *United States*, 352 U.S. 476 [1957]) is not an indication that it is suitable reading. But some of the best literature of the twentieth century has been written by men who develop themes around the use of sex which are truly Christian. No more powerful book illustrating the meaning of the Catholic priesthood has been written than Graham Green's *The Power and the Glory*, the story of a drunkard priest who fathers an illegitimate child. The reader of this novel is brought to an intense awareness of the meaning of redemption in a sinful world. The parents of teen-agers must take an interest in their children's reading, and attempt to influence it toward materials which are similarly valuable artistically and educationally.

CHAPTER 8

PREPARING FOR MARRIAGE

Dating

Every culture has to evolve some method of mate selection. The American system, commonly called dating, has distinctive characteristics. It allows a great deal of freedom in association with persons of the opposite sex once the young adult has passed the age of puberty. Institutional control from the family, the school, and the Church is kept at a minimum. Educational, cultural, religious, racial, and economic factors are still important determinants of young adult associations, but their influence is more subtle than formerly. The freedom of association which characterizes American dating patterns can create problems in the task of choosing a husband or wife. While they are dating, most young people are only vaguely aware that their experiences are preparing them for the work of selecting a partner in marriage. Many of them are too wrapped up in themselves to prepare effectively for this great choice. With our prolonged system of education many nineteen- and twenty-year-old men and women are still looking inward and trying to formulate some picture of their identity and person. Many psychologists have pointed out the basic personal insecurity which American college students have. This insecurity, this search for identity, often leads young people into disappointing social relations with persons of the opposite sex.

In an intensive effort to prove that "I am somebody," many young people turn dating into a kind of competitive search for meaning. If a man doesn't call for a second date within a week or two, a woman will make herself miserable because she assumes that he found something very wrong with her.

When a boy is interested in a girl, he will become enraged if she dates someone else because he assumes she finds him a bore. Not infrequently young people who are in no way thinking of marriage will go through a period of exclusive steady dating in which each will assert a personal claim over the other. This relationship often explodes in an emotional crisis after which the two may not even talk to each other. This is undesirable because in such dating patterns a young person is not learning to deal with other human beings in a mature, enjoyable, and developmental manner.

The best form of dating would be one in which young people learn the techniques of communication. Dating should educate a person to have concern for the neighbor, to learn how to relax with those who are sexually different, to appreciate, however gradually, the qualities one would want in a mate. To achieve this, a young man or woman must forget about play acting or image projection. TV's commercials try to persuade that hair products and deodorant are the prime factors in successful dating, but associations which do not make a young person a more mature and communicative human being fall far short of their potential.

The Choice of a Husband or Wife

The Fathers of the Second Vatican Council suggested that, while selection of a marriage partner must be the final and free choice of the individual, the parents should prepare their children for this great choice:

> Parents or guardians should by prudent advice provide guidance to their young with respect to founding a family, and the young ought to listen gladly. At the same time no pressure, direct or indirect, should be put on the young to make them enter marriage or choose a specific partner.[1]

---

[1] The Pastoral Constitution on the Church in the Modern World, art. 52.

Some parental guidance will be possible if the channels of communication between parent and child have been nourished and strengthened over the years until they have developed into a mature, confidential, and trust-filled relationship. But parents must realize that a twenty-two-year-old man or woman is not a child. Dialogue must be based on mutual respect for the intellect, emotions, and opinions of the young person. The latter must recognize the seriousness of choosing a husband or wife. In choosing a life partner, a Christian believes that he is selecting a life partner with whom he will carry out one of the great sacramental acts of Christ in his Church. It is not a choice to be made lightly.

Romantic attraction is certainly a factor in making this choice. The mysterious factors which attract a given man to a given woman have never been adequately explained. Frequently, this attraction seems to have no rational basis. Psychologists have suggested that it may be a combination of unconscious or subconscious motivations: recognition of one's egotistical ideal, bodily attraction, compensation for personal inadequacies, or transfer of incestuous desires.[2] Yet Rudyard Kipling probably gave the best definition of romantic attraction when he said "It's just it." Kipling may have also suggested a key to romance when he wrote that "the first proof a man gives of his interest in a woman is by talking to her about his own sweet self. If the woman listens without yawning, he begins to like her. If she flatters the animal's vanity, he ends by adoring her."[3] Whatever the basis for romantic attraction, it is a part of life. The beautiful description of the desire of the maiden for her lover in the fifth chapter of the Canticle of Canticles and the use of romantic imagery by Saint John of the Cross in the *Spiritual Canticle* show that the romantic inclination can be even of religious value. But romance cannot be the determinate factor in mate selection. A male may experience romantic attraction for many women, and vice-versa. Such attraction is not love. The Christian believes that love doesn't strike a person like a thunderbolt, but is a virtue to which a person knowingly commits himself.

When a young man and woman meet and find that they are sufficiently attracted to each other to consider marriage, what kind of an analysis should they make of their situation? It is both impossible and undesirable for anyone but the couple themselves to decide if marriage is for them. Nevertheless, some effort to evaluate certain qualities which

---

[2] See Chapter 2 of I. Lepp, *The Psychology of Loving* (Baltimore: Helicon, 1963; paperback: New York: New American Library [Mentor-Omega], 1963).

[3] *Under the Deodars*, "The Education of Otis Yeere."

are essential to marriage in both partners is in order. Maturity, that is, the ability to see life in a realistic perspective, is the most basic of conditions precedent to a successful marriage. The alcoholic, the spendthrift, the dreamer who is perpetually dissatisfied with a world which never measures up to his fantasies — such persons are not prepared for marriage. Almost as vital is honesty. If a person discovers that either he or his prospective mate is not able to trust one another, he should conclude that their relationship cannot succeed in the unity of marriage. Simply pronouncing the vows of marriage will not change a dishonest way of dealing with one another. The ability to compromise is the basis of any successful interpersonal relationship. Compromise does not mean surrender of one's own will power but learning how to keep an open mind in order to arrive at mutually satisfactory solutions to daily problems. Ability to communicate is a quality which is invaluable in marriage. Perfect communication between any human beings is impossible, but growth in marital love will witness an ever-deepening power of understanding between husband and wife. The continuing inability of a couple to deal with each other except at a superficial level is a danger sign to a couple contemplating marriage. A general cultural and educational equality is not always vital, but it does aid the ability to communicate. Economic factors must be considered and frankly discussed. Extremely important is a general community of agreement on basic moral attitudes. This does not mean that unity of cult is necessarily vital because even members of the same denomination may have incompatible moral views. Many decisions requiring moral considerations on sex, education of children, money, etc., must be made in marriage and only a very foolish couple would think fundamental moral attitudes are unimportant. Age is not usually very important, unless the disparity is great.

Many young people are led to believe that they will "fall into love." Love is a dedication and consecration to another which is built consciously, not something which just happens. In choosing that other person, a young man or woman must consider factors which will be conducive to the building of a loving relationship.

CHAPTER 9

THE ENGAGEMENT AND THE
CELEBRATION OF THE NUPTIALS

The Formal Agreement to Marry

When a man and woman decide on marriage, it is customary for them to formalize their intentions by some public expression. This is called engagement. The public announcement may be by newspaper, at a party, or through a family dinner. It may also be through the celebration of the Betrothal Rite of the Roman liturgy. This word, betrothal, which is frequently used to indicate the public announcement of engagement should not be confused with the word betrothal used in the New Testament to describe the relationship between Joseph and Mary. The Israelites recognized the importance of preparing for marriage, but economic factors demanded that the family-arranged marriage take place as early as possible. The boy and girl would marry, but the marriage would not be consummated until both bride and groom were more mature. Mary and Joseph were in this period of betrothal, which usually lasted twelve months, when the annunciation occurred. The modern betrothal signals the beginning of a period of preparation for marriage preceding the nuptial pledges. This betrothal rite has its origin in the Roman law. Long before the time of Christ the Romans had developed a formal ceremony in which a man and woman would exchange public promises to marry several months before the nuptials.[1] At first a weighmaster would direct a ceremony in which uncoined brass was exchanged between the couple as a sign of their promise. When coinage became more common, a coin would be broken and one half given to each. Eventually, an exchange of iron or gold rings marked this *consensus sponsalitus*.

In the third and fourth centuries the Roman betrothal passed into the Christian liturgy. The solemn, liturgical betrothal also borrowed from Germanic practices of ceremonial exchanges which surrounded the familial marriage decision and from Jewish ritual as well as from Roman sources. Several fourth-century Fathers, including St. Augustine and Pope St. Sirius, wrote of the liturgical betrothal as if it were quite common. The form used varied throughout the Church, but several common factors eventually emerged by the medieval period: a public statement by the parties of their intent to marry, the presence of a clerical and two lay witnesses, a blessing of the engagement ring, and the recitation of scriptural readings and prayers which challenged the couple to prepare seriously for the sacramental vocation of marital love. Eventually, this custom fell into disuse, probably due to its abuse in the espousal of infants and the extremely juridical approaches to betrothal which developed under Canon Law.

However, the practice of "ratifying in solemn manner the engagement . . . (and) entreating the blessing of the Church on the proposal" (from the Allocution of the Betrothal Rite) is experiencing a revival in the American Church. Stripped of the legal consequences of former centuries, the solemn betrothal gives a couple the opportunity both to proclaim publicly their belief in the holiness of Christian marriage and to experience the encouragement which the words of the rite can provide.[2]

---

[1] The Roman law alluded to was the *Jus Civile*, not the better known *Jus Gentium* which was eventually codified under Justinian in A.D. 534. The *Jus Civile* stressed the "mancipatio," the public agreement to enter into a contract carried out by a well established ritual. This is typical of primitive contractual law.

[2] For the complete text of the Betrothal Rite, see P. Weller, *The Roman Ritual* (Milwaukee: The Bruce Publishing Company, 1964), p. 297.

The Purpose of Engagement

Engagement serves two purposes. First, it is a period of trial. It is not uncommon for a couple to break off the engagement if they discover that there is only minimal probability of success for their proposed marriage. Almost half of the engagments announced in the United States do not result in marriage. In a society which gives young people almost total freedom in choosing a spouse, with little familial influence on the choice, this use of engagement as a period of trial by the couple is necessary.

A second purpose of engagement is preparation for marriage. The celebration of the nuptials will not automatically cast a golden aura of success around a couple. A successful marriage requires conscious dedication, and, if the months preceding the marriage are used properly, the couple will be building the bridges which are necessary to a successful union. The channels of communication will begin to open, or close, with the first joint attempt to formulate plans for marital life. If habits of untruthfulness, self-centeredness, and sullenness, are characteristic of an engaged couple's dealings with each other, such habits will likely continue in marriage. The period of engagement is a time when a couple should learn to build forms of honest and personal communication with each other.

Engagement should be a time of ever-increasing personal contact and cooperation between the man and woman. Each cuts off dating relationships with others and concentrates on the other. This is the time to explore basic attitudes on the great problems of life. Common interests should be determined. As the engagement progresses, a normal healthy couple will find their physical and psychological longing for union taking on ever new and deeper forms. This is the reason that an engagement should not be prolonged beyond the time when their relationship is ready for total union. Marriage manuals will attempt to define what is an unreasonably long engagement, but this must always be determined by the totality of circumstances in which the couple find themselves.

The preparation for the celebration of the nuptials is an important part of an engagement. Arranging the plethora of details which normally surround an American wedding is a good opportunity for developing mutually compatible working habits. Many grooms do not participate in these preparations. This is undesirable, because joint preparation for the wedding establishes a working rapport which can be invaluable in the first months of marriage when innumerable details of family life must be worked out together. The wedding must be planned out in stages since postponing the major details until the last few weeks will leave the couple tired during the first months of marriage when there are enough problems of adjustment to communal life. Since the bride's family normally pays most of the expenses of a wedding, they will have the primary say about details. However, it is desirable that both families cooperate with the couple; this cooperation can create an atmosphere of mutual understanding between in-laws which can only help a young couple in their years of marriage.

During the engagement, the couple should learn to seek competent help and advice. The pre-marital medical examination is not yet generally accepted in the United States, except in the few states that require it by law. The doctor can give a couple good advice about sex and reproduction. The examination may reveal some factor which will affect sexual union and of which the couple should be aware. He can also discuss familial or hereditary illnesses, as well as personal medical problems, in an atmosphere of calm, professional analysis. A Christian couple will want to discuss any mental or physical factors which may affect their union or their children. There are so many misconceptions about such matters as epilesy, breast cancer, diabetes, congenital defects, etc., that a couple should get proper medical advice rather than depending on the "advice" of family and friends. Almost all states require a blood test prior to the issuance of the marriage license in order to determine if either party is carrying a venereal disease. But the advice of the physician should be sought on the much discussed Rh Factor. Many engaged people have the information necessary to make the evaluation of how the Rh Factor relates to them but never take the time to seek advice. The consequences for childbearing if the woman has Rh positive and the man is Rh negative, or to a lesser extent if the reverse is true, make it only sensible that a couple would not enter marriage totally in the dark if they suspect problems in this area. Learning how to face problems both analytically and courageously is a quality a couple should start to develop early.

Marriage in a complex socioeconomic world brings with it many legal and monetary consequences. The need for insurance on the breadwinner, problems of taxation, the ownership of property, the desirability of an expandable will which carries out the plans of the couple, the purchase of real or personal property: these and many other legal and economic factors are not uncommon in the preparation for marriage. The moment that the engagement announcement appears in the paper a host of salesmen merchandising everything from dishes to insurance will descend on the couple. The need for experienced and competent advice in all of these things is apparent. A trustworthy friend may be able to give such advice. A couple should not be afraid to seek the help of an attorney if a particularly complicated problem arises. If trust property is involved, if the couple are purchasing a home or taking a long-term lease on an apartment, if help is needed in interpreting an insurance policy or drawing a will, etc., an attorney is a trained professional who will be able to protect the interests of the couple in these matters. After marriage, he will be able to give continuing advice, and will be of invaluable help in making decisions to adopt children, obtain a mortgage, in tax problems, etc. Having a knowledgeable person who is totally committed to their interests can be most helpful to a couple.

Engagement should be a time in which the couple build a working relationship with future in-laws. Visits should be made to each other's homes. There is no reason why inter-family relationships should not be cordial, but sometimes a little effort is required to achieve this. However, both parents and future in-laws must be convinced that the new family which will be born through marriage is not simply an alter ego of the existing families. Many parents are reluctant to let go of their children's lives after these children have entered marriage. A few hours' observation of divorce proceedings will convince anyone of how debilitating parental interference can be on a young marriage. Direct, financial subsidy from parents to married children, sometimes camouflaged under continuing "gifts," is a growing phenomenon. With the possible exception of limited temporary aid for specific and absolutely necessary purposes, such as continued education, parental support will inevitably destroy the freedom of decision which every married couple need in order to achieve a family life of their own. The parents of a couple must be subtly made aware of their children's determination to establish their own family life after marriage. The couple should honestly talk over their relationship to the families during the engagement so as to minimize confusion and misunderstanding after marriage.

Many dioceses require an engaged couple to attend a Pre-Cana Conference. These conferences center around discussions of particular aspects of marriage. The lecturer or discussion leader at a given conference may be a medical doctor, a lawyer, a married couple, a theologian, a psychologist, etc. Depending on the speakers, these conferences can be valuable. Yet many college educated Catholics, who have taken detailed courses in the theology of marriage, sociology, and/or biology find them repetitious and superficial. A few Catholic colleges have introduced campus Pre-Cana Conferences so that engaged couples in the student body can participate in a program which is geared to their background and needs. Many dioceses are attempting to organize programs which can be adjusted to meet the needs of diverse couples. The Pre-Cana Conference, admitting its weaknesses, is generally a valuable experience for the engaged couple. The Fathers of the Second Vatican Council encouraged the establishment of similar organizations devoted to programs of instruction in marriage throughout the church universal.[3]

The Celebration of the Nuptials

The nuptials, from the Roman term *nuptiae* which indicated the sealing of the engagement contract by marriage, refers to the mutual expression of the marital pledge between the parties. This expression of consent to the marriage is both the marriage contract and the sign of the Christian sacrament. "The sacrament of matrimony is the symbol of the union of Christ and his Church . . . the efficient cause of matrimony is mutual consent, ordinarily expressed through words and representing a present intent."[4] The expression of marital consent is frequently, by custom and law, surrounded with religious and civil ceremonies. Very early in the history of the Church, Christians developed the custom of expressing their pledge in a religious ceremony which would signify the sacramental ideal. In the year 305 St. Ambrose of Milan could speak of this practice as quite ordinary in the Latin Church: "The ceremony of marriage should be sanctified by the priestly veiling and blessing."[5] In the same century the custom seems to have taken on the force of law in the Eastern Church. About A.D. 375 St. Basil would write that "If a marriage is contracted without the approval of those in authority, it should be considered fornication."[6] Today Canon 1094 binds Catholics to celebrate their nuptials in the presence of the

---

[3] *The Pastoral Constitution on the Church in the Modern World*, art. 52.
[4] *Instruction on the Sacraments*, Council of Florence, Denz. 1327.
[5] Letter to Vigilius.
[6] Letter to Amphilochius on the Laws of the Church.

bishop or the pastor (or a delegated cleric) and two other witnesses, except in unusual circumstances. It is not the three witnesses, however, who act for the Church; they are present to attest to the effect which the marriage will have on the whole body of the Church. It is the bride and groom who perform the sacramental act of Christ; it is the bride and groom who again bring Jesus actively into his Mystical Body in sacrament, in the sense that they act for the whole Body in performing this Christ act. The priestly witness needs the consent of the parties to proceed with the diverse ceremonies surrounding the nuptials: "The rite is always to honor the requirement that the priest assisting at the marriage must ask for and obtain the consent of the contracting parties."[7]

Since Catholics believe that the Breaking of Bread is the great sign and cause of Christian communal unity in Christ,[8] it is customary to celebrate the nuptials of marital unity within the Mass. "Matrimony is normally to be celebrated within the Mass."[9]

The fathers of Vatican II encouraged the use of local customs in the marriage celebrations. "If certain locales traditionally use other praiseworthy customs and ceremonies when celebrating the sacrament of matrimony, this sacred Synod earnestly desires that these by all means be retained."[10] Some of these customs are highly symbolic representations of Judeo-Christian ideas about marriage. The bride is handed over to the groom by her father as a sign that the man and woman have left their parents to become one flesh with each other. The couple will exchange rings which symbolize the totality and permanence of their gift to each other:

> Bless, O Lord, this ring, which we bless in your name, that she (he) who shall wear it may keep true faith unto her (his) spouse, and may abide in Thy Peace.

The great sacramental acts of Christian Unity are brought together as the bride and groom communicate together from the chalice.

Frequently, the nuptial celebration is followed by a social festivity among the friends and neighbors of the couple. It is natural that great social joy should permeate the community when a new family is born.

---

[7] *Constitution on the Sacred Liturgy*, art. 77.

[8] 1 Cor 10:17; the fathers of the Second Vatican Council called the Eucharist "a sacrament of love, a sign of unity, a bond of charity." *The Constitution on the Sacred Liturgy*, art. 47.

[9] *The Constitution on the Sacred Liturgy*, art. 78.

[10] *Ibid.*, art. 77.

Occasionally, some narrow-minded person complains about these festivities, and it has not been unknown for the priestly witness to offend the couple by failing to attend the celebration and offer the grace. This is paradoxical conduct if set against the example of Christ. Jesus not only attended the social festivities which followed the marriage of a family friend, he even provided the alcoholic beverages for the occasion.

The business of weddings is big business in the United States, where more than a billion dollars a year is spent on the various ingredients of American weddings. Much of this money is wasted. Bridal consultant firms will arrange every detail of the wedding. However, the total expense will be increased considerably if a firm is hired and the couple will lose the once in a lifetime opportunity to arrange their own wedding. Learning to buy, to shop, to work out plans together can be a great experience. The couple will want to surround their nuptials with details and ceremonies which speak their own thoughts about marriage. Beyond the fact that this means some middle line between filling out papers in a clerk's office and a Rose Bowl extravaganza, the external dedication to the life of marital love should be the result of personal loving attention by the couple.

A SELECT BIBLIOGRAPHY FOR PART II

An asterisk (*) indicates works available in paperback editions.

Bier, W. (ed.), The Adolescent: His Search for Understanding (New York: Fordham University Press, 1963).

Connell, W., The Adolescent Boy (Chicago: Fides, 1958).

Dresen-Conders, H., The Psychology of Sex Instruction (New York: Sheed and Ward, 1963).

Dufoyer, P., The Choice of a Husband (New York: Alba House, 1964).

―――― The Choice of a Wife (New York: Alba House, 1964).

Duvall, E., The Art of Dating (New York: Association Press, 1958).

*―――― Love and the Facts of Life (New York: Popular Library, 1963).

―――― Why Wait Till Marriage? (New York: Association Press, 1965).

Filas, F., Sex Education in the Family (Englewood Cliffs, N. J.: Prentice Hall, 1966).

Greeley, A., Letters to Nancy (New York: Sheed and Ward, 1964).

*Haley, J., Accent on Purity (Notre Dame: Fides, 1960).

*Hettlinger, Richard, Living With Sex: The Student's Dilemma (New York: The Seabury Press, 1966).

Imbiorski, W., The New Cana Manual (Oak Park: Delaney Pub., 1957).

*Kelly, A., A Catholic Parent's Guide to Sex Education (New York: Hawthorn, 1962).

*Marshall, J., Preparing for Marriage (Baltimore: Helicon Press, 1962).

*McManus, W., *Marriage Guide for Engaged Couples* (Glen Rock: Paulist Press, 1961).

Odenwald, R. and Newland, M., *How You Were Born* (New York: P. J. Kenedy, 1962) (sex educ. in pre-teen years).

*Oraison, M., *Learning to Love* (New York: Hawthorn, 1965).

Reuss, J., *Modern Catholic Sex Instruction* (Baltimore: Helicon, 1964).

*Sattler, H., *Parents, Children, and the Facts of Life* (New York: Image Books, 1956).

Spellacy, F., *Courtship and Marriage* (Boston: St. Paul, 1961).

Thomas, J., *Looking Toward Marriage* (Notre Dame: Fides, 1964).

*Willke, J. C., *The Wonder of Sex* (Cincinnati: Hilty, 1965).

Winch, R., *Mate Selection* (New York: Harper and Bros., 1958).

PART III

LIVING CHRISTIAN MARRIAGE:
THE VOCATION TO COMMUNION

INTRODUCTION TO PART III

COMMUNICATION AS THE EXERCISE OF
CHRISTIAN COMMUNION

The apostles and friends of Jesus believed that they were united to each other by a bond of *Koinonia*. This Greek word, which appears frequently in the New Testament, is translated into English as communion or fellowship. St. Luke used it to describe the life of the first Christians: "they devoted themselves to the Apostles' teaching and fellowship, to the breaking of bread" (Acts 2:42). St. John the Apostle told the Christians that he preached the word of God in order that they might share in this bond: "that which we have seen and heard we proclaim also to you, so that you may have fellowship with us; and our fellowship is with the Father and with his Son, Jesus Christ" (1 Jn 1:3). When the apostle Paul was in chains at Rome, he wrote a letter to his friends in the Church at Philippi. In the letter St. Paul gave some dramatic examples of the wonderful bond: "I hold you in my heart, for you are all partakers with me of grace, both in my imprisonment and in the defense and confirmation of the gospel" (Phil. 1:7).

In some way the Philippians are benefited by Paul's suffering; but the mysterious bond which unites Paul and his friends also works to his benefit. "I know that through your prayers and the help of the Spirit of Jesus Christ this will turn out for my deliverance" (Phil 1:19). This bond of common life among the followers of Jesus, perhaps best known to most Catholics as the "Communion of the Saints," means that the Christian by his vocation is dedicated to an ever-deepening union with Christ as He lives in the fellowship of the believers. Paul urges this on the Philippians: "Only let your manner be worthy of the gospel of Christ; so that, whether I come and see you, or am absent, I may hear of you that you stand firm in one spirit, with one mind striving side by side for the faith of the gospel. . . . So if there is any encouragement in Christ, any incentive of love, any fellowship in the Spirit . . . complete my joy by being of the same mind, having the same love, being in full accord and of one mind" (Phil 1:27 to 2:21).

If marriage is an act of Christ in his Church, it must be related in some way to this building of the Christian fellowship. Since their vocation consecrates husband and wife primarily and immediately to the good of each other, it is in their relationship to each other that they will experience and build fellowship. Paul identified fellowship in the Spirit with one-mindedness, and the married couple must seek to achieve ever deepening communion through a community of understanding. To grow in communing requires a constant concern for the other, a concern which leads to persistent efforts to reach out and contact the other at every level. The communication needed for successful communion does not mean talk; the couple who are always concerned about each other will develop both verbal and nonverbal means of communication. But successful communication is not easy to achieve or maintain. It requires a conscious effort to understand each other's moods, emotions, worries, and responses to diverse problems and stimulations. Communication requires truthfulness; total, constant truthfulness between two people who must deal with one another day after day is one of the most difficult of human virtues. But unless it is present, communion is impossible. To the extent that it is absent, the couple have ceased to live in a fellowship and have reverted to the individuality of their premarital lives.

Indifference to the neighbor is rapidly becoming a hallmark of urban life. Because indifference, which means lack of concern, is so destructive of love, it must be one of the worst vices a man can develop. Many marriage counselors are convinced that the indifference which becomes so obvious on city streets exists in numerous homes. It is not a vice which one develops consciously. It begins in little things: the husband's preoccupation with a job which ever so slowly becomes the purpose of his life; the wife's concern for the children which gradually leads her to think of her husband simply as the provider for family needs. The Christian couple will determine that indifference will not overtake their relationship. Contrary to the pious little ditty, Christian marriage does not mean praying together in order to stay together. Staying together is not an ideal; growing together in communal love is the ideal.

In the play *Other People's Hearts* Gabriel Marcel presents a picture of a marriage in which there seems to be a true communion between husband and wife. As the play progresses, it becomes apparent that the union is more apparent than real. There is much talk, but no communication. The husband has come to assume that his wife's ideas, ambitions, and needs correspond exactly to his. His personality has become the personality of the marriage. This is the antithesis of marriage; to find only one's own ego instead of communion. To prevent it, a couple must constantly seek to communicate with each other. The Christian vocation to communion requires dialogue. Just as communication is the key to the ecumenism which seeks to rebuild the fellowship of Christian unity, it is also basic to the communion of marital lovers.

CHAPTER 10

THE SIGN OF COMMUNION

The Eucharist and Sex: Signs and Causes of Unity[1]

Christian communion or fellowship is not a purely metaphysical phenomenon. The New Testament speaks of a physical cause and sign of fellowship among the believers. "The cup of blessing which we bless, is it not a communion in the blood of Christ? And the bread which we break, is it not a communion in the body of Christ? Because there is one loaf, we who are many are one body, for we all partake of the same loaf" (1 Cor 10:16–17). Every Christian has a union of fellowship with his fellow members of the Body of Christ; the physical sign and cause of this fellowship is a common loaf of bread, broken by all the members of Christ. This is why the breaking of bread is at the center of ecclesial communication.

It is precisely at this point that the similarity between the Church and marriage comes sharply back into focus. The symbolic and effective unity which the Church finds in the Eucharist is paralleled in marriage

---

[1] The likeness between the role of sex in marriage and the role of the Eucharist in the Church has frequently been the subject of theological discussion. The most famous is the comparison drawn by St. Robert Bellarmine in *De Controversis*, III, De Mart., II, 6. A recent example is found in the talk given by Bernard J. Cooke at the University of Notre Dame Conference on Population and published in *The Problem of Population*, Vol. III, p. 27; cited in the bibliography.

by the representative and actual union which husband and wife find in sex. Sexual union in marriage is like the loving physical contact, complete involvement, and recommitment to unity with the loved one which the believer experiences in eating the communion Bread. St. Augustine described the Eucharist as the "sacrament of love, the sign of unity, the bond of charity,"[2] a description which would approximately reflect the role of sex in Christian marriage. This unifying power has rarely been more beautifully described than in the dialogue between the bride and bridegroom in the Song of Solomon:

(BRIDEGROOM):

How graceful are your feet in
    sandals,
O queenly maiden!
Your rounded thighs are like jewels,
    the work of a master hand.
Your navel is a rounded bowl
    that never lacks mixed wine.
Your belly is a heap of wheat,
    encircled with lilies.

Your two breasts are like two fawns,
    twins of a gazelle.
Your neck is like an ivory tower.
Your eyes are pools in Heshbon,
    by the gate of Bath-rab'bim.
Your nose is like a tower of
    Lebanon,
      overlooking Damascus.
Your head crowns you like Carmel,
    and your flowing locks are like
      purple;
    a king is held captive in the
      tresses.

How fair and pleasant you are,
    O loved one, delectable maiden!
You are stately as a palm tree,
    and your breasts are like its
      clusters.
I say I will climb the palm tree
    and lay hold of its branches.
Oh, may your breasts be like clusters
    of the vine,
    and the scent of your breath like
      apples, —

and your kisses like the best wine
    that goes down smoothly,
    gliding over lips and teeth.

(BRIDE):

I am my beloved's,
    and his desire is for me.
Come, my beloved,
    let us go forth into the fields,
    and lodge in the villages;
let us go out early to the vineyards,
    and see whether the vines have
      budded,
whether the grape blossoms have
    opened
and the pomegranates are in bloom.

There I will give you my love.
The mandrakes give forth
      fragrance,
    and over our doors are all
      choice fruits,
new as well as old,
    which I have laid up for you,
    O, my beloved
        (Song 7:1–13).

---

[2] *On the Gospel of St. John,* Tract 26, 13, 6.

While the Christian can best see the communal aspect of sex by likening it to the Eucharist, it is interesting that the Old Testament envisions a similarity between sex and the communion with God which Israel found in the Covenant. The marriage act of sexual intercourse is described in the book of Genesis (4:1) as a "knowing" of each other, an intimate discovery of the other. The same word is used by the prophet Hosea to describe the union which Israel should plan with God: "my people are destroyed for lack of knowledge" (Hos 4:6). The intimate communing of men with God and the love expressed between a husband and wife were then recognized as like each other even before the breaking of bread, but this clarified the mystery.

A Knowledge of the Physiological-Psychological Functions of Sex Can Contribute to Growth in the Fellowship of Christian Marriage

Before a Christian participates in the fellowship of the breaking of bread, he is expected to study and think about this great mystery. In its centuries of accumulated wisdom the Church has learned that catechetical instruction makes for more meaningful use of the sacrament of unity. The same is true of marriage. The couple who have some understanding of the sign of their unity will be better able to use sex as an effectuation of their communion in love. St. Paul tried to give the Christians at Corinth an explanation of the bread they broke at the communal meal in order that they could achieve greater unity in its eating (1 Cor 11:17-34). Similarily, married Christians will seek to understand the physical and psychological elements of sexual union in order that they may grow in the mutual expression of love.

Sex is the particular form of communion which distinguishes marital love from other forms of fellowship. It is a wonderfully complex thing, and like the Incarnation, human sex is the ennobling of materiality. Over the centuries, thoughtful Christians have grown in the realization that the material existence of man has been touched to the point of redemptive sanctification by the reality of Jesus. Unfortunately, theologians have not given sufficient attention to the similar condition by which the incarnation of love into sexual union makes the marital community approach to the God-like. Partially, this is due to puritanical feelings which have persisted among many Christians and which caused a certain uneasiness in speaking and thinking about the processes of sex. This is inexcusable if measured against the great debates and discoveries about the human condition which have enlivened the centuries since the Council of Chalcedon defined the meaning of God becoming man. Christian couples, and the best theological minds in the Church must learn to discover the fact of sex as a beneficial force in human life. Knowledge of this great mystery by which a man carries out God's creative act and shares in the fellowship of Christ's redemptive love can only contribute to the ability of Christian spouses to achieve the fullness of their vocation.

Basic Facts of Sexual Communion

The following discussion does not attempt to set out all of the things man knows about sex. To do so would be impossible even in many volumes. An attempt is made to present some basic functional aspects of sex which can help a person to begin developing an awareness of how sexual communion works. Growing up in the expression of marital love through sex is a highly individual experience to each couple, but knowledge of these functional aspects is desirable even before marriage. This discussion will not follow a manual approach, for no one can lay out a precise step-by-step plan for successful sexual communion any more than one could write a minute-by-minute program for a successful life. But the reader is urged to consider carefully the implications which the different aspects of sex discussed may have for the life of Christian marriage.

Sex is communal in nature. In the Bible it is not the sexuality of the male alone which is blessed as a power by which human life reflects the divine; it is the union of male and female which receives the blessing (Gen 1:28). But because male and female sexuality are different and complementary they can best be analyzed separately.

Sex in the Male

Masculine sexuality is much more localized physically than is female sexuality. Physical sexual power and response are centralized in the organs located at the bottom of the body trunk between the legs. These organs consist of the testes and the penis. The testes are located in a protective pouch called the scrotum. This pouch is outside and hanging from the body trunk because the functions of the testicles require a temperature lower than that of the body. The testicles produce both spermatozoa and the hormone which is responsible for male physical characteristics. This hormone, testosterone, affects not only the physical appearance of the male, but his way of thinking as well. Its quantity will affect the way a man reacts to women and the overall development of what is called the male psyche. Knowledge of this function should help diminish the idea that human physical sexuality relates exclusively to reproduction, an assumption which has been implicit in the writings of some theologians.

Spermatozoa are produced in the testes in great numbers, about 250,000,000,000 maturing each month. A single spermatozoon is about five- to six-hundredths of an inch in length. Its forepart, or head, carries the materials which will convey the hereditary factors of the male should it fertilize a female ovum. The body of the spermatozoon forms into a tail which moves back and forth in order to propel it forward. This propulsion is aided by other factors in both the male and female. A gray liquid, the seminal fluid, helps carry the spermatozoa along. A male lubricant is also produced in connection with the expulsion of the spermatozoa from the man's body. This is complemented in the female by a vaginal lubricant which helps both penetration and the movement of the sperm through the reproductive organs of the female.

Before being placed in the body of the woman, the spermatozoa are carried from the testes through a series of canals and into an organ called the epididymis where they achieve final maturity and are stored. The matured spermatozoa are moved from the epididymis through a large tube called the vas deferens at the end of which they blend with the seminal fluid, after which they enter the prostate gland. From the prostate, these substances move into a long canal which runs through the penis. This canal, the urethra, is the canal by which the spermatozoa are enabled to leave the male's body through the hole at the end of the penis. While the urethra is also the means by which the male bladder is emptied, the urinary and sexual systems are separate from each other. During ejaculation, the bladder is closed off and urine cannot mix with the seminal fluid.

There are various estimates as to how long spermatozoa will survive outside the protective temperatures of the male sex organs. A common estimate is between fifteen and thirty hours, depending on the degree of acidity in the woman's sexual organs. The greater the acidity, the more quickly the spermatozoa will die. Medical science has still not determined how long the spermatozoa retain their fertilizing power, although such power is probably lost before the sperm itself dies.

The penis is the exterior male organ through which the urethra runs.

It is a shaftlike organ which hangs limp in front and above the scrotum. Under sexual stimulation, the vessels in the penis fill with blood and the organ becomes hard and erect. This condition, called erection, enables the male to insert the penis in the vagina of the female.

The excitement produced by erection causes muscle spasms to occur in the male. These spasms are felt in the genitals, at the base of the back and in the legs, and produce a brief but intense feeling of pleasure which is called orgasm. These spasms cause the release of spermatozoa and seminal fluid and help move these substances through the urethra and out the hole at the end of the penis. This expulsion is called ejaculation. Usually an ejaculation results in the expulsion of several hundred million spermatozoa, although the number may be considerably less if a prior ejaculation has occurred recently.

It is commonly thought that male sexuality is almost exclusively physical. This is untrue. The fact, female sexuality is in some respects less influenced by the mind than is the male (although it must not be thought that the woman's psyche is unimportant to her sexual response). Memory is a particularly important factor in male sexual response. The erection center of the brain is important to the creation of impressions which influence the build-up of sexual feelings in the husband. Mental inhibitions, whether produced by guilt feelings, a puritanical education or some physical cause such as alcohol, diminish the probability of physically-psychologically successful sexual consummation on the part of the male.

Sex in the Female

From the physical point of view sex in the woman is more generalized than in the man. The expressly sexual organs are more spread out in the female, more parts of her body are open to sexual stimulation, and she experiences a reproductive cycle unknown to the male; sexual arousal is slower than in the male. Yet a woman's sexuality is complementary to that of her husband's. The ovaries are the counterpart of the male testes. Unlike the testes, they are located inside the body trunk, but they serve the same functions. The hormone responsible for female physical and psychological characteristics, estrogen, is produced by the ovaries. As was observed in the discussion of the testes, this hormonal production indicates that, even physically speaking, sexuality does not relate exclusively to reproduction. The second function of the ovaries is the maturation of the female reproductive cell, the ovum or egg.

Before she is born, a baby girl has thousands of primordial ova in her ovaries, and she will not produce any more during her life. Only a few hundred of these will mature and be available for fertilization by a male spermatozoa. Once a girl reaches puberty, a matured ovum will be discharged from the ovary during each menstrual cycle, and this will continue until the menopause period of middle age. This discharge is called ovulation, and pregnancy cannot occur unless the discharged ovum is fertilized during the few hours it will survive apart from the ovary. Since most women ovulate between eleven and fifteen times a year, it is apparent that the human female is infertile (incapable of conceiving a child) on all but a few days in each year. The two ovaries generally rotate in discharging ova, one ovulating in one cycle and the other in the next. However, one ovary may discharge several consecutive ova while the other remains inactive. It is also possible that in one cycle both ovaries might discharge ova or one ovary might discharge two or more ova; either of these conditions creates the possibility that multiple fraternal (as distinguished from identical) conceptions may occur.

Each of the ovaries is located near the end of a fallopian tube. These tubes are several inches long, and it is into them that, by some combination of factors not yet fully understood, the discharged ovum is attracted. In the tube the ovum will either be fertilized by a male spermatozoon or die within a period variously estimated at up to twenty-four hours. While ovulation is occurring, an important related development is taking place in the uterus. The fallopian tubes empty into the uterus, which is a muscular cavity about two or three inches long. The muscular walls of the cavity are firm and hard, but when a new cycle of ovulation begins a soft lining begins to develop. This makes the walls of the uterine cavity about four times thicker than they would be immediately after a menstrual discharge. This uterine lining is meant to protect a child who has been conceived because the fertilized ovum (zygote) will pass down the fallopian tube and attach itself to the wall of the uterus. If a child is not conceived in the hours following ovulation, the wall which has been built up in the uterus becomes unnecessary. The lining will then break down and pass from the body. This passage of the uterine lining is called menstruation.

Because there are not normally any visible signs of ovulation,[3] most

---

[3] A few women feel a slight pull, popularly called "ovulation ping," when an ovum is discharged. Ovulation is accompanied by a small vaginal discharge in a very few women. Most women do not even have these inadequate signs of ovulation.

people refer to the ovulatory cycle as "the menstrual cycle." It should be apparent that this terminology is unfortunate because menstruation is only the aftereffect of an ovulation which did not result in pregnancy. As long as this fact is understood, menstruation might be of some value to a couple who are attempting to estimate the probable time of ovulation. At present, there is no way that ovulation can accurately be predicted, but a record of menstruations may indicate that ovulation is occurring with such regularity that a fair estimate of the time of fertility could be made. Of course, some women do not experience ovulation with sufficient regularity that menstruation would be any help in estimating the time of probable fertility. The fact that the next ovulation has occurred X number of days after a prior menstrual discharge for so many consecutive months (this being the cause of the regularity of menstruation) does not insure that ovulation will occur at a similar time in the cycle which begins next. In spite of these deficiencies in the use of menstruation as a guide in predicting ovulation, every woman who expects to be married or has recently been married should keep a record of menstrual discharges and length of cycles. This information may some day be of limited help to a couple who desire to conceive a child or practice a rhythm method of birth limitation.

There are two means by which some women attempt to determine when ovulation has occurred. Since ovulation is accompanied by a slight rise in body temperature, a daily recording of temperature may aid a woman in knowing that she has ovulated. Ovulation is also accompanied by the presence of glucose in the top of the vaginal cavity. Tapes which will change color when they contact glucose have been developed. The innate problems with both the basal temperature method and the fertility tape method are that neither is a perfectly accurate guide (since other factors beside ovulation might induce the conditions on which their effectiveness is premised) and they can only tell after-the-fact when ovulation has occurred.

The uterus opens into the vagina through the cervical canal. The vagina is a cavity surrounded by muscular walls, about 3 to 5 inches long. Normally the walls rest lightly against each other. But when this cavity serves its functions, it is capable of expanding in both width and length. The male penis is inserted into the vagina during intercourse, and the interaction between the penis and the vagina is the primary cause of orgasm in both the husband and wife. The lubricants produced by the woman under sexual stimulation aid intercourse. A second purpose of the vagina is its function as the birth canal. In the process of birth, the muscular wall of the vagina expand and contract sufficiently to permit a baby to pass through. The vagina is also the means by which the menstrual discharge passes from the body.

Through the centuries, poets and theologians have devoted much attention to the hymen. This thin membrane is a partial covering just inside the vagina. Its presence has sometimes been called the sign of physical virginity. As such it has been overrated, because its absence is hardly a sign that a woman is not a virgin. It is sometimes broken long before marriage in innocent circumstances. The hymen exists only to keep undesirable substances out of the vagina before puberty. If it does exist at the time of marriage, it will be broken at the time of the first penetration, causing a slight uncomfortableness and perhaps a little bleeding. The rare case of a hymen which is so thick as to prevent penetration is one of the good reasons for a premarital medical examination. A minor operation can cure this condition.

The external female organs are located in two entirely distinct parts of the body, on the chest and at the bottom of the body trunk between the legs. The opening to the vagina is found in the latter position. This opening is protected by the vulva or labia which are two folds of skin running back to front on each side of vaginal opening. The outer fold is called the major labia because it is larger; the inner fold is called the minor labia. These folds also enclose the opening to the urethra through which the bladder is emptied. The labia are somewhat sensitive to sexual stimulation; in front of the opening to the urethra they also enclose the clitoris which is extremely sensitive to such stimulation. The clitoris, like the male penis, fills with blood and becomes hard and erect under sexual excitement. Along with the vaginal rubbing produced by intercourse, stimulation of the clitoris is an important, if subordinate, factor in female orgasm.

The breasts are located in an entirely different part of the body from the other female sex organs, but are a vital part of a woman's sexuality. The breasts of a man are only slightly erogenous, but those of the mature woman become erect and pleasurably sensitive to contact through the stimulation of marital foreplay. In the unified totality of function by which the Creator has blended sexual reproduction, the breasts serve the additional purpose of providing nourishment to newborn children. This function is not an incidental one, it is a part of woman's sexuality. In a nation where cow's milk is almost a cult, the value of human milk is greatly neglected. The minimizing of allergies, the ease of digestive adaptation, vitamin balance, greater protein content, the suppression of further ovulation, and the psychological value of breast feeding are some of the advantages of this mode of nursing the young child.

It was suggested above that the psyche of the male is quite important in his sexual response. In the female, memory and intellect are not so important in determining sexual responses, although they do have a role to play. In the woman, emotion is more important than in the man. Because of her tendency toward an intuitive feeling for life, she is often able to relate sexual experience to emotional content of the total relationship better than can the male.

Growth in Communion Through Sex

John Henry Cardinal Newman once remarked that growth is the only evidence of life. This is certainly true of marriage, for the vocation to which the couple have committed themselves is one of growth in the life of love. Sex should contribute to that growth. Human sexual union is not easily perfected from every point of view: the physical, emotional, psychological. It is only in a union openly dedicated to growth in love that it can slowly approach perfection. The marriage manuals which identify sexual perfection only with mechanical technique easily mislead people into a narrow view of human sexuality. Expression of love and experience of fellowship in marital sexual union differ radically from promiscuous sex in precisely this: the former is part of a total relationship in which the couple find limitless opportunity to grow up in the use of a God-given power of love. Perfection of technique is a part of this growth, but in accord with the complexity of the human personality, marital sexual love can open the door to growth in every dimension of the husband's and wife's being. A leading Catholic philosopher, Michael Novak, has beautifully expressed some of the potentialities which marital sexual love holds for the life and persons of the husband and wife:

> It unifies the couple; it often restores their spirits and their energies; it heals wounds; it sends out rays of harmony into all the moments of the day; it sets a standard of trust and communion to which they must live up in all their other actions; it nourishes, judges, and expresses their mutual bond.[4]

---

[4] "Closing the Gap Between Theology and Marital Reality," *The Commonweal*, Vol. LXXX, No. 11, p. 344 (June 5, 1964).

Devoting a lifetime to fulfilling these potentialities is a part of the marital vocation. It is also part of the spouses' Christian vocation by which they are committed to building the fellowship of Christ.

Modern man is not limited to spatial proximity. In communication with others, he has spanned continents and oceans with electronic devices. In the future, he will span planets and even solar systems. But for all this man has never found an adequate substitute for the sense of touch as a means of communication. Touch is limited by spatial proximity, but it is one of the most effective means by which fundamental human feelings and emotions are communicated. Communication by electronic devices is limited to letters, words, and sentences. The only sense which makes man's body known to himself and to others is the sense of touch. And touch, far from denoting only physical contact, has the capacity to convey to the mind impulses which the mind then translates as thoughts or emotions. Inasmuch as man experiences data for his understanding and judgments through his body, physical objects have always had the capacity to convey meaning more readily than have slogans or ideals.

In a mother-child relationship, touch and proximity are vital, and they increase in intensity and totality as the relationship proceeds. A mother when holding her child for the first time will hold him so gently, and far out from her own body. The next time she holds him, she will want to undress him and run her fingers over his body to feel his wholeness. Later, she will enfold him in her arms and mold him to the shape of her own body. Similarly, a mother with one child will be much more hesitant and anxious about handling her newborn than will a mother with ten.

In a love relationship between a man and woman, the pattern is similar. As both sexes gradually become aware of each other, they are hesitant in learning to touch one another, and for a long time, permit each other only to look. There is for the young adolescent the traumatic experience of the first time holding hands, the first kiss. They then start the whole process of touch all over again when their bodies fuse and become one and share in the process of creating life. To "have sex" with and "make love" to another person is the ultimate to which they can go in touch communication.

Touch has the capacity to convey to the mind impulses which are translated into meaning. The mother, by bringing the child close to her, is conveying to the child that she has accepted him, likes him, and wants to have him near her. The man and woman in the marriage act also tell each other these things, and their communication is more profound than the mere words could ever be, because through their mutual act of love they experience one another as both mind and body. Because of the totality of giving involved, their union is by nature permanent. Once anything is given totally, it can never be recalled, since there is nothing remaining of its former existence to recall it. A gift once given freely to a friend is not a gift anymore, but a possession of that friend.

Since the last barriers of defense erected by touch have been broken down in sexual union, the couple now also find it easier to communicate on the more superficial level of the mind alone, without even touching at all. This is because they have learned to identify completely with each other and have truly become one in both body and spirit. The objection that any two people could engage in the sex act and have this same deepness of communication and identification with each other because of the binding force and closeness of the sex act itself is heard more frequently today. Can this be?

To answer this, we must first consider the nature of man. Some of man's acts are purely animal, such as eating, sleeping, elimination of waste. The physical drive to reproduce is purely animal, and is necessary for the evolution and continuation of the species. But man is also rational, meaning that his actions are based on a totality of correct judgments. Could it not be possible, then, for man to reason that since the act of love is physically pleasurable and relaxing, why not indulge in it whenever the person, place, or time strikes the fancy? Many people have reasoned this way. But what they fail to realize is that loving is not knowing but something beyond it. "Love never ends — as for knowledge it will cease" (1 Cor 13:8). Knowing something merely demands that a person experiences, understands, and judges an object or idea or situation correctly, but loving demands a gift of oneself. To know that someone is good, to love him demands total commitment and involvement with him. To become a complete human person one must necessarily make this transition from knowing to loving.

The person who has made the necessary loving commitment to another in marriage cannot help maturing into a vital and responsible person capable of experiencing his total sexuality. Sex, as a vehicle of love, is not merely something we do, but what we are. Happiness within a good sex-love relationship permeates the whole life, and overflows to the being of the two and becomes one flesh. As the married couple become more aware of each other, they also become more aware of themselves, and are constantly seeking to better themselves for the loved one. One thing is certain and that is this: two people have brought each other closer to the Love that created the world through their own joy in love.

CHAPTER 11

MARRIAGE AS A SHARING OF GOD'S CREATION OF HUMAN LIFE

The Good of the Procreation of Children

The Christian believes that children "are a heritage from the Lord, the fruit of the womb, a reward. Like arrows in the hand of a warrior are the sons of one's youth. Happy the man who has his quiver full of them" (Ps 127:3–5). The ancient words of the Psalmist were recently reaffirmed by the fathers of the Second Vatican Council:

> Marriage and conjugal love are by their nature ordained toward the begetting and educating of children. Children are really the supreme gift of marriage and contribute very substantially to the welfare of their parents. The God himself who said, "It is not good for man to be alone" (Gen 2:18) and "who made man from the beginning male and female" (Mt 19:4), wished to share with man a certain special participation in his own creative work. Thus he blessed male and female saying: "Increase and multiply" (Gen 1:28).

Hence, while not making the other purposes of matrimony of less account, the true practice of conjugal love, and the whole meaning of the family life which results from it, have this aim: that the couple be ready with stout hearts to cooperate with the love of the Creator and the Savior, who through them will enlarge and enrich his own family day by day.

Parents should regard as their proper mission the task of transmitting human life and educating those to whom it has been transmitted. They should realize that they are thereby cooperators with the love of God the Creator, and are, so to speak, the interpreters of that love. Thus they will fulfill their task with human and Christian responsibility. With docile reverence toward God, they will come to the right decision by common counsel and effort.

They will thoughtfully take into account both their own welfare and that of their children, those already born and those which may be foreseen. For this accounting they will reckon with both the material and the spiritual conditions of the times as well as of their state in life. Finally, they will consult the interest of the family group, of temporal society, and of the Church herself.[1]

To the Christian, children are not simply an incidental aftereffect of marriage. They are a blessing from the Creator who has given them a magnificent opportunity to participate in creation. (See Jer 1:5.) Children are part of the Creator's plan for man's achieving holiness in the union of one flesh: "Has not the one God made and sustained for us the spirit of life? And what does he desire? Godly offspring. So take heed to yourselves, and let none be faithless to the wife of his youth" (Mt 2:15). Children, responsibly begotten or adopted, and responsibly educated are a blessing to husband and wife (Gen 1:28). The reality of this blessing will be analyzed from the viewpoints of conception, adoption, and education.

Conception, Pregnancy, Birth

Human life begins with the fertilization of a female ovum by a male spermatozoon well up into the fallopian tube. The spermatozoon penetrates the ovum and fuses with its nucleus. At this moment, the new life has all the paternal and maternal elements its parents can physically communicate to it. With fertilization the new life secretes a protective

---

[1] *Pastoral Constitution on the Church in the Modern World*, art. 50. As to childless marriages, the bishops added: "Marriage is not instituted solely for procreation. Rather, its very nature as an unbreakable compact between persons . . . demands that the mutual love of the spouses, too, be embodied in a rightly ordered manner, that it grow and ripen. Therefore, marriage persists as a whole manner and communion of life, and maintains its value and indissolubility, even when offspring are lacking."

wall which prevents any more spermatozoa from entering. It then begins to break down into a multi-celled being. The life will take about a week to move along the fallopian tube toward the uterus. The uterine wall is developing; when the new life reaches the uterus, it will implant itself in the wall.

An important hormonal development is also taking place in the body of the woman. The female hormone estrogen, which was mentioned in the preceding chapter, is produced in greatest abundance in the time just preceding ovulation. With the discharge of the egg from the ovary, another hormone, progesterone, is produced and estrogen declines. It operates better to prepare the uterine wall for implantation of the egg, to suppress further ovulation[2] and is related to the preparation of the breasts for the production of milk.

Even after the life has implanted itself in the uterine wall, the couple do not yet know that their love has borne the fruit of new human life. In the next few weeks, however, certain signs will begin to appear. None of these are absolute indicators, but when some of them appear, a couple should have a doctor make an A-Z or HCG test to determine the matter conclusively. The enlarging of the breasts, failure of the menstrual discharge to occur, increased urination, nausea and/or a feeling of fatigue are among the signs of pregnancy which a woman will notice. When a pregnancy is known, a Christian couple will do everything reasonably possible to protect the life of the child they have conceived. The fathers of the Second Vatican Council speak of this as a moral duty: "From the moment of its conception life must be guarded with the greatest care."[3] But the clear thinking Christian parent will not see this simply in terms of duty; rather, it will be an opportunity to participate ever more fully in the work of Creation through nourishment of the great gift of love which is human life. Medical attention is an important part of this care. For thousands of years the human race was unsuccessful in fighting off the probability of prenatal death and injury. Today, medical science has at least minimized this danger, and a couple should try to take advantage of these advances. The danger of prenatal death and injury can be diminished by medical examination, treatment, and advice. A conscientious doctor will give directions on matters of diet, hygiene, intercourse, work activities, travel,

---

[2] The use of progestin as a progesterone substitute to suppress ovulations is the basis of the birth control pill discussed in the next chapter.

[3] Supra, n. 1, art. 51.

exercise, and will provide no little amount of encouragement to the first-time parents.

It is frequently asked if the little cluster of cells which attaches itself to the uterine wall is human. It is clear that from the moment of conception on the new life has all the genetic elements it will ever possess. The Christian believes that human life is something sacred, assumed by God himself in the Incarnation, and that the newly conceived life must be treated as human. This statement of moral obligation would not be necessary for the Christian parent who is steeped in the love for life which flows from the mysteries of Creation and the Incarnation. The Christian parent will love and respect the life which has blessed their love, and do everything possible to assure it a chance to develop into a mature human person.

Even when parents do everything they can to protect and nourish the newly conceived life, a miscarriage during the first months of pregnancy is still possible. The possibility of miscarriage is about one chance in ten, with a greater likelihood in the first pregnancy than in subsequent conceptions. If a couple have done their best to preserve the life, they should not feel guilty about a miscarriage. As Christians, they will know that the seemingly unexplainable must have some role in the Father's divine governance of the universe. Medical science offers a tentative solution to the occurrence of miscarriage in the explanation that the discharged embryo or fetus is probably seriously abnormal or would not be able to live through the full terms of pregnancy.

About two weeks after conception the new life is called an embryo, and would be just barely large enough to be seen by the naked eye. After about four weeks, the brain and digestive system have begun to develop and the heart starts to beat. The embryo is about one-fourth of an inch long. After six weeks the arms and legs and a disproportionately large head have formed, the embryo being about one-half inch long. The embryo is floating in liquid, called the bag of waters, a condition which will continue until birth. During the early days in the womb, a vital organ, the placenta, develops. This organ grows in the uterine lining. The umbilical cords runs from the placenta to the navel of the embryo. The placenta is vital to the embryo because it performs such life functions as filtering out waste, bringing in oxygen and food, and keeping the blood of the mother and child separate. Because it is expelled after the child has left the womb, the placenta is popularly called "afterbirth."

From the eighth week on, the life is called a fetus. In the next months, fingers and toes are formed, hair begins to grow on its head, and the external sex organs are developed. At four months a fetus is about four and a half inches long. In the next month or two the mother often notices light movements. The mother's abdomen increases noticeably in size. The child frequently begins to change position during the fifth and sixth month. Sometime during the last months he will finally assume one position, usually head downward, and remain so until birth. The last months of pregnancy are uncomfortable for the mother, but are usually a time when husband and wife intimately share plans and feelings in tender expectations. The father's role may be limited to occasional heartbeat soundings and saving his wife a few steps, but his mental attitude and willingness to share the joys and difficulties of these months through dialogue are vital ingredients of the marital love which is so open to growth in this period. But if there are other children in the family the father's role at this time can really be expanded. He ought gladly do things his wife customarily does, and older children too ought to be led to see what they can contribute.

Birth is the process by which the child passes from the body of the mother. The causes which set it in motion are not known. The mother may experience light contractions for some weeks before birth. When the contractions become quite regular and frequent, this is normally a sign that labor is beginning. As birth approaches, the contractions will come closer and closer together. Two especially important things happen at the beginning of the birth process. The bag of water breaks and the opening of the cervix between the uterus and vagina begins to widen. The time of labor varies in different women and in different pregnancies. At one time it was customary to isolate husband and wife in separate little rooms during labor; most modern hospitals recognize that these hours are a time for a man and woman to be together. The hours of labor can be a time of pain, but they are also a time of expectation. Jesus described the birth of a child as a time of joy, and the Christian couple will know that in the birth of their child they are experiencing the fruit of God's blessing. The Psalmist expressed this happiness by singing: "Blessed is every one who fears the Lord — your wife will be a fruitful vine within your house, your children shall be like olive shoots around your table. Lo, thus shall the man be blessed who fears the Lord — may you see your children's children. Peace be upon Israel" (Ps 127:1, 3, 4, 6).

Adoption

During his ministry, the apostle Paul used various phrases to express man's continuing relationship to God through Christ. One of his strongest expressions was a comparison of this relationship to the adoption of a child. "You have received a spirit of adoption, as sons, by virtue of which we cry Abba! Father! The Spirit himself gives testimony to our spirit that we are the Sons of God. But if we are sons, we are heirs also; heirs indeed of God and joint heirs with Christ" (Rom 8:15-17).[4] There is a gospel basis for the apostle's enthusiasm: The Son of God told men that they should become "sons of your Father who is in heaven" (Mt 5:45). Theological writers have always found in the Pauline notion of adoption to divine sonship a favorite theme in the Christian life. Yet even those who have attempted to develop a theology of marriage have given little attention to adoption itself.[5] If the practice of taking a child and making him one's own is so noble that it reflects the Fatherhood of God, then it must be one of the greatest human acts of love. The Christian knows that God's act is one of love; the apostle John told the first century Christians:

> See what manner of love the Father has given us, that we should be called the children of God . . . beloved, we are God's children now (1 Jn 3:1-2).

Adoption is one further way that a married couple can stand in the image of God, for in this action they imitate the love of the Father for all men.

An adopted son can never be the conceived child of his parents, just as man can never be God. Paul calls man an adopted son of God because, while he cannot achieve divinity, man can share in that which Jesus has by nature. As the Son of God, Jesus has knowledge of God: "Father, the world has not known thee, but I have known thee" (Jn 17:25). The adopted son of God can share in this inheritance of Jesus: "I will not leave you orphans (Jn 14:18) . . . in that day you will know

---

[4] Confraternity translation.

[5] Arthur Mirgeler has written: "We must note with surprise the fact that adoption plays an embarrassing role in Western Christianity, occurring in families without natural offspring, and not — as in pre-Christian Rome — a constructive role in society. This is all the more astonishing in view of the teaching of Christian theology that man's basic quality through grace is that of being an adopted child." *Mutations of Western Christianity* (New York: Herder and Herder, 1964), pp. 140-141. The *Decree on the Apostolate of the Laity* cites adoption first in the recommended list of activities of the family apostolate (art. 11).

that I am in my Father, and you in me, and I in you (Jn 14:20) . . . and this is eternal life, that they know thee the only true God" (Jn 17:30). The parallel to human adoption is striking. A couple gives a child the opportunity to share their family life. This child does not carry their genes, but in every other respect he becomes the son of the adoptive parents. To adopt Paul's terminology, the child becomes the "heir" of the couple, entitled to the full inheritance of a child they would conceive themselves. His status as heir is not only the legal right to inherit material goods in case of parental intestacy, it is the right to stand as beneficiary of the years which the adopting couple will devote to his well-being.

There is an unfortunate tendency to circumscribe human parenthood in the narrow context of physical conception. Undeniably the conception of a child is a magnificent participation in the creative act of the Father; but the practice of adoption should never be denied the same accolade. The parent in the fullest sense of the word is the one who accepts the long-term responsibility of loving, dedicated, educational attention to the work of helping a child achieve natural and supernatural maturity. This is true whether the child is conceived by the parents or adopted by them. As the adoptive parents work to help their child mature, they will be giving him an intellectual and moral life which fills out his physical existence. These parents will leave something of themselves in the child. It may be metaphysical, but it is real. In the act of divine adoption the Father is giving something of himself to man; "he has granted us the very great and precious promises, so that through them you may become partakers of the divine nature" (2 Pet 1:4). The same opportunity is open to the adoptive parent.

In spite of New Testament use of adoption as a reflection of the Fatherhood of God, some Christians speak disparagingly of the practice. Some very crude persons imagine a mark of illegitimacy on adoptable children. Un-Christian racial prejudice prevents a full development of the practice in the United States. Indeed, organizational structures within the Church have often tended to favor institutionalizing adoptable children rather than influencing the community to see the practical and religious values of adoption. Certainly, the adoption of a child is a serious and responsible act, just as is the conception of a child. But it is an act which Christians should commit themselves to support. The cultural, educational, physical, and moral advantages of family life over institutional life were not scientifically demonstrated until the twentieth century, but the Christian has long known that adoption is one means by which a married couple can put themselves more deeply into the image of the Father.

Developing Human Life Through Education

Marriage is holy because it gives man a share in the creative life and activity of God. To a dogmatic theologian, creation represents something more than the bringing of things into existence. From the writings of the early Fathers, through the medieval summas, to the tracts of the contemporary theologians the practice of associating divine providence with the act of creation has been constant. The statements of the Councils have also related the two mysteries, as if they were simply two dimensions of the same truth. The First Vatican Council, in its statement on God as Creator described him as "governing the things he has created, his power extending from end to end, disposing all things with gentleness."[6] To achieve its purpose, creation requires divine governance: "it would not be fitting for the goodness of God to be responsible for bringing things into existence without also giving them their ultimate perfection."[7] It has been emphasized earlier in this volume that marriage is holy because it is a participation in God's creative activity. The application of the word procreation to marriage has not been limited to the instituting of new life; the stress has been on the need for growth in the new life of marital love, on the lifelong enriching of the new redemptive life the couple share in the sacrament. This consideration, that creation requires attention to development as well as the production of life, must be carried over into a consideration of the procreation of children. To conceive or adopt a child is only the beginning of the procreative work of the parents. If they are to be fully the image and likeness of the Creator, husband and wife will spend years nourishing, protecting, developing, and helping the child reach maturity. To put it simply, education is a vital part of the procreation of children.

Parents Are the Primary Educators

At birth the child has only the limited experience of the womb. Six years later, the child will be a functioning human being, with many

---

[6] *Dogmatic Constitution on the Catholic Faith*, April 11, 1870, Denz. 3006.
[7] St. Thomas Aquinas, *Summa of Theology*, First Part, Q. 103, a. 1.

of his basic life attitudes already formed. During these years the one ever-constant source of guidance, direction, and information is the parent. Viewed from this perspective, it can be appreciated that the parent is usually *in fact* the primary educational influence on the life of the child during the most important educational years. Yet, this is not the only reason that the parent is described as the primary educator. This description is simply the definition of the responsibility a man and woman take on themselves when they conceive or adopt a child. Because they participate in the mystery of procreation with each other, the father and mother must think of education as the fulfillment of that mystery. Amid the moral collapse which accompanied the rise of Nazism, Pope Pius XI tried to recall the German people to a realization of basic Christian principles. One of the most important of these was for parents to reassume the role of primary educators, a role which the National Socialists were gradually taking over through various devices.

> Conscientious parents must become aware of their duties in education for they have the first and primary right to develop the life which has been given to them by God . . . we send an especially concerned greeting to Catholic parents. Their exercise of their God-given responsibilities in education is now the subject of a terrible struggle; their work could not conceivably hold greater consequences for the future . . . never forget this: God has given you alone the full responsibility for your children — from this responsibility no power on earth can separate you.[8]

The parents may ask the civil and/or religious community to help them carry out their responsibilities, but the moral duty of education rests with them as primary educators.

The term education is here used in its broadest sense. It is not limited to influencing the intellectual development of the child. The educational work of the parents must reach out to the whole personality of the child, and help him to advance toward maturity on the physical, emotional, affective, moral, and social levels as well as in the formation of the mind. So broad is the educational work of parents that mistakes will inevitably be made. Conscientious parents will constantly rededicate themselves to the work of educational development and will critically analyze the effect which their actions are having on children. The parents must frequently discuss together such matters as discipline, the child's social development, the value of different toys and children's books, punishment, nutrition, and emotional disturbances. Only through

---

[8] Encyclical Letter, *Mit Brennender Sorge*, March 14, 1937, art. 37 and 47, A.A.S., 29.

explicit communication with one another can they minimize the probability of mistake.

The aim of parental education is to help the child achieve human maturity. The free and fully developed human being, capable of achieving his destiny in the creative-redemptive plan of God — this is the goal the parents must strive to attain. Education does not mean making the child dependent on the educator; it does not mean turning the child into an image of oneself. The parents will want to give the child an ever-growing independence, and will want to show him how to use his freedom by building a power of ordered judgment as to himself, his fellowman, and his final destiny. To accomplish this kind of education requires a great deal from parents. It is always easier to impose conformity on a child from without than to help him develop an inner sense of self-discipline and direction. But this is the difference between a master and an educator. To help the child achieve an ordered judgment which is the touchstone of human maturity, the parents must allow a balanced combination of freedom and patient guidance in the life of the child. The child must be allowed to touch, see, smell, and hear a great deal of God's creation. Freedom of exploration and discovery for the child will cause inconvenience for parents, but the wholesome development of a wondrous curiosity and respect for the mystery of creation demands it. In the discussion of sex education, the need for building a confidential and trusting relationship between parent and child was stressed. Such a relationship is indispensable if the parent is going to help the child put the universe he discovers into perspective. He will learn that he can trust his parents to answer his questions honestly. He will seek to understand the reasons which underlie the values about life which the parents express. The maturing child will not develop a blind emotional loyalty to parental viewpoints, but if he finds that these viewpoints relate reasonably to the view of life he is developing, then he will emulate them in his thinking. There is nothing wrong with a child taking his parents as behavior models, but the acceptance of the model must be based on the inward conviction that parental behavior is worth imitating.

Earlier, in Chapter 7, we indicated that most children exhibit a certain pattern of inquisitiveness and development in their sex education. This is not so true in overall educational development. This fact, and the realization that the emotional, physical, moral, and intellectual needs of each child are so different make a detailed analysis of educational principles for parents impossible and undesirable in a general textbook. Nevertheless, a few general considerations can be made, and from these the reader can go on to further reading and thought which will help him form convictions on the matter of parental educational responsibilities.

One tendency which parents must be careful to avoid is the desire to possess the child, as if he were simply an alter ego. Psychologists have pointed out that in every parent there is an egocentric instinct to treat a child as if he were an extension of oneself. The extreme case of parental possession is the "mama's boy," but there are less obvious forms of the tendency. The parent who praises his child as a "good boy" should examine himself to determine if the qualities which merit the applause are not just accommodations to the parent's convenience. Is the child "good" because he is quiet, because he doesn't get his clothes dirty, because he doesn't annoy adults or get in their way? If so, there is danger that the parents are communicating a very superficial set of values to the child — one which is rooted in the desire of the parent to make the child conform to his convenience. Praise is an essential element of a successful parental-child educational relationship, but it should be given for substantive qualities and accomplishments which result from the child's own efforts. Politeness is one of these substantive qualities, but it should be a politeness which is formed by a growing respect for one's fellow man — not unthinking conformity to adult standards. Another form which parental possessiveness can take frequently appears during the secondary school and collegiate years. It is the subtle communication of parental ambitions to the child. Anyone who has been on a college campus for a time can attest that this is a reality of life today. Parents should give vocational guidance, but must avoid crossing the line which exists between guidance and the imposition of parental ambitions.

Pope John XXIII wrote that "every human being has a natural right that his person be respected."[9] Respect for the person of the child is essential to education. This respect must exist at every level of the child's personality. If an emotion such as anger results in anti-social conduct, the latter must be reproved; a parent-child talk should bring out if the feeling of anger was justified. If the child expresses an absurd idea or plan, it should not be dismissed out of hand or ignored, the parent must strive to understand the basis for the thought and help the child

---

[9] Encyclical Letter, *Pacem in Terris*, April 11, 1963, Part I, A.A.S., 55.

relate it to reality. The right of the child to experience human emotion and to learn how to judge and plan — this is what the parent must encourage.

The religious education of the child is of special concern to the Christian parent. Religious education does not mean the arbitrary imposition of moral imperatives on children; neither does it mean the development of habitual rituals with religious overtones within the family. Religious education means a progressive understanding of the mysteries of creation and redemption. This progression requires that the child be helped to understand God, Christ, man, and moral duty in accord with his age and educational development. The natural curiosity of the child which the parent seeks to exploit in every educational endeavor must be used in religious formation.

For example, there is a growing tendency to leave basic instruction in the sacraments to the parents; the latter should present the sacraments not as formal rituals but as a participation in the redeeming work of Christ. The child's curiosity about water should lead the parents to explain the life-giving qualities of water for plants, for animals, for man. When the child has grasped this, the parent can extend the idea to the life of the redeemed creature: we use water to symbolize the life in which a man shares when he enters the body of Christ. The use of ordinary things to teach religion to a child is essential if the latter is going to successfully relate religion to the vision of life he is developing.

The School: Delegate Educator

To many people the word education is a synonym for academic schooling. In a nation dedicated by law and philosophy to academic education, the school is, in fact, a major element in educational development. Yet schooling is not the totality of education, and the fact that the child is in school does not mean a cessation of the parents' work. The entrance of the child into school merely creates new dimensions in the parents' labor. The first of these is the choice of the school. The right to choose the school is corelevant to the parental duty as primary educator: "Parents, who have the first and inalienable duty and right to educate their children, should enjoy authority's freedom in the choice of school."[10] In choosing the school, parents should not make decisions in a hap-

---

[10] Declaration on Christian Education, art. 6.

hazard way but should weigh all the known circumstances to determine in which school the child will receive the best physical, emotional, moral, and intellectual development. If a Catholic school is available, and is suited to the work of education in the judgment of primary educators, this should be the choice.

After the school has been chosen, the parents must keep informed of what is happening there. Conscientious parents will form or join organizations through which school authorities will communicate information about policy and practices. It is unfortunately true that in many parishes the pastor and the principal are reluctant to make public information about teacher qualifications, curriculum, textbook evaluation, and finances. Catholic teaching on the primacy of the parental rights in education is so ancient and well-developed that such secrecy is inexcusable. The parent has a right to know how the education of his child is being accomplished in the school. Once the parent has some idea of what is happening in the school he can coordinate the child's family responsibilities and opportunities to his academic development. Home and school should not be unrelated worlds in the educational development of the child.

The Catholic school should contribute to the religious education of the child. The parents must evaluate whether this is, in fact, happening. The parent has several indicators which demonstrate the quality of religious education in the school. The first such indicator is the instructor. Who teaches religion? Is he or she a trained catechist or does every teacher "handle" a religion class regardless of qualification? The teaching of religion to a class of children is such a delicate thing that more harm than good is inevitably done by the unqualified teacher. A catechist must not only know what is valuable to a child in religious phenomena, he must also have sufficient knowledge of child psychology that he can actually enter the children's world and there share the mysteries of creation and redemption in a meaningful way. One more characteristic of the Catholic teacher was provided by the Second Vatican Council. It must be the dominant characteristic. "United in charity, let teachers in Catholic schools be penetrated by an Apostolic spirit, let them bear witness to Christ, the unique teacher."[11]

Special liturgical practices in the parish should be adapted to the needs of children and religious practices in the home should accord with the progress which the child is making in his education. Long,

11 *Ibid.*, Art. 8.

highly formal religious rituals do not contribute to religious education. The texts used should reflect the tremendous advances in applying educational psychology to religious formation. A parent who has attended college probably is sufficiently sophisticated to determine if the texts are kerygmatic in approach or just tidied up versions of the Baltimore Catechism. The competent catechist is usually most cooperative in explaining to parents why a particular text was chosen and how it is used.

If the Catholic school is to carry out its role as delegate educator successfully, the entire Catholic community must support its work; this support includes a healthy and honest criticism of poor practices. The work of Christian education is too important to be second rate. The fathers of Vatican II asked "both pastors and people to devote themselves to the purpose of making the Catholic school an ever-better means"[12] to Christian education. The Catholic college graduate should be committed to this improvement. The Catholic college and university should support it through programs to prepare qualified teachers of religion for the secondary and primary schools. The parent must be able to feel confident that when he commits his child to a Catholic school he has a "partner"[13] who is competent to help his child achieve human and Christian maturity.

---

[12] *Ibid.*, Art. 10.
[13] *Ibid.*, Art. 8.

CHAPTER 12

RESPONSIBLE PARENTHOOD,
MARITAL LOVE, AND
FAMILY PLANNING

The fathers of the Second Vatican Council stressed that "human life and the task of transmitting it . . . have a bearing on the eternal destiny of man."[1] It is apparent from what has been said so far in this text that the Christian reverences the power which enables him to procreate human life and desires to use it in accord with God's will as far as he can know it. The will of the Creator as to the relationship between the expression of marital love through sex and the power of physical procreation has long been sought by Christians. In his classic study of this problem, Dr. John T. Noonan has shown that sterilization, contraception, and abortion have been consistently rejected by Christians,

---

[1] *Pastoral Constitution on the Church in the Modern World*, art. 51.

although for different reasons in different ages.[2] The consideration of this question has reached a high point in the contemporary Church due to the press of overpopulation, the development of new forms of fertility control, changing family patterns, and a growing emphasis on the existential aspects of the theology of marriage. It is a confusing, emotional, and difficult problem, but the response of the Christian Church to it is one of the most important touchstones of the relevance of Christianity to modern life. From the discussion and analysis of the problem will come, hopefully, a clarification of the values of human reproductive power, an important contribution to the theology of marriage, and even a more precise understanding of the magisterium of the Church. This brief chapter of necessity only touches on the bare outline of the problem; the interested reader is urged to begin an examination of the voluminous material available on the subject.[3]

One dimension of the problem is terminology. The term *birth control* is popularly used in the United States. It came into being as a synonym for contraception at a time when the latter word was considered obscene and could not be used in matter sent through the mail. Later, the meaning of birth control broadened to include other forms of birth limitation. It means so many diverse things that the term causes more confusion than clarification. *Birth limitation* and *family planning* are clearer terms, for they indicate the practice of avoiding indiscriminate reproduction without specifying the means used. The careful person will achieve clarity by using a precise word when he is speaking of a particular means of birth limitation (contraception, anovulant pill, rhythm, etc.) rather than these general terms. The phrase *responsible parenthood* has become popular among Catholics; it indicates the duty of parents to act as thoughtful human beings in the reproduction and education of children as they should in every activity of life.[4]

---

[2] *Contraception* (Cambridge, Mass.: Harvard University Press, 1965).

[3] A popular but accurate summary of contemporary views is Dorothy Dunbar Bromley's *Catholics and Birth Control;* three paperback books entitled *The Problem of Population* present an easy-to-read series of position papers delivered at the University of Notre Dame. These and the other books listed in the bibliography of Part III will at least introduce the reader to the literature on the subject. Publication such as *Commonweal, Jubilee, Ave Maria, America,* and the *National Catholic Reporter* generally will keep him abreast of current books and developments.

[4] See "Responsible Parenthood," *The Commonweal* (entire issue), Vol. LXXX, no. 11, June 5, 1964. The term first gained public usage when it was used as the title of an important statement on birth limitation issued by the World Council of Churches in 1959. The full text of the statement is found in *The Ecumenical Review* for October, 1959, p. 85.

Basic Principles of Family Planning

The conception of a child is an awe-inspiring responsibility. The Catholic believes that when he brings a child into the world he is committing himself to the long task of helping that child achieve humand and Christian maturity. It is an eminently social responsibility, beginning with the community of husband and wife, reaching out to the new life which is the child, affecting the physical, moral, and psychological well-being of other children in the family, and ultimately enriching or disturbing the good of the community by the success or failure of the parent's educational work. Few human actions are so important. Acting responsibly requires planning; neither the indiscriminate breeding of children who cannot be properly raised in human dignity nor the purely selfish use of sexual power are Christian ideals.

What are some of the factors which are relevant to the responsible transmission of life? Mere physical comfort of the husband and wife obviously should not be the sole basis of a decision in this area; man is not created and redeemed to achieve maximum physical comfort. A couple whose love is so shallow that it is not capable of desiring a growth in the family it creates are hardly living the *agapē* in their marriage. Ability to lead a family life in which parents and children may "avoid as much as possible misery and uncertainty"[5] is quite relevant to family planning. This does not mean that parents must be able to give their children all of the comforts, goods, and economic advantages which magazine and television advertising proposes are necessary to the "good life." It does mean that the size of the family unit must bear a reasonable relation to its educational, social, and monetary needs. Dr. John J. Kane has pointed out that the patterns of family life which prevailed at the turn of the century, with its emphasis on a large number of children, cannot be followed by most contemporary parents who wish to meet their responsibilities.[6] In a technical society, the responsible raising of children creates more intensive demands, both quantitatively and qualitatively, than those made on parents in a rural and agricultural-oriented society. It is apparent that only the couple are in a position to evaluate these demands in the light of their own situa-

---

[5] Pope Leo XIII, Encyclical Letter *Rerum Novarum*, art. 13, A.S.S., 23 (1890–91).
[6] John A. O'Brien, "The Population Explosion Demands World-Wide Action," *The Christian Century*, Aug. 28, 1963, p. 1051. Father O'Brien quotes the opinion of Kane and other scientists on the implications of current sociological conditions for the practice of birth limitation.

tion and personalities. The distinguished moralist Bernard Häring has urged parents to frame their decisions by this question: "How many children can we rear in such a way that they will not only become able citizens, but also active members of the kingdom of God and heirs of eternal life?"[7]

Another factor which must be considered by a couple who want to act responsibly is their own health. There are some couples for whom five children in four years constitute a refreshing plunge into the mainstream of life; for another couple such a situation would be a mental and physical disaster. The latter couple are not necessarily immature — in all areas of life one encounters activity which for some is normal and for others a dangerous stress-situation.

Eugenic considerations may also be important. The probable transmission of defects may reasonably cause a couple to decide on the limitation of their family.[8] Finally, the misery, crowding, war, and hunger predicted by demographers if world population continues to grow at present rates require the Christian to consider what he can do to create a suitable environment for human existence. The limitation of births may be one contribution he can make to the good of the human community.[9]

The Means of Birth Limitation

The Pastoral Constitution on the Church in the Modern World counseled that "sons of the Church may not undertake methods of

---

[7] "Responsible Parenthood," Marriage, Vol. 46, No. 7, July, 1964, p. 24,

[8] Eugenic problems constituted one of the grounds cited by Pope Pius XII for the practice of family limitation, Address of Oct. 29, 1951, A.A.S., 43. Every married person should try to obtain some knowledge of genetic inheritance. Ashley Montagu's Human Heredity (New York: New American Library, 1960) (Mentor paperback), gives a most readable presentation of the basic realities of genetics and a list of heredity clinics which might be helpful to a couple seeking advice. See also Amram Scheinfeld, The Basic Facts of Human Heredity (New York: Washington Square Press, 1961, paperback). Although eugenic considerations are a reasonable basis for family limitation, there can be no justification, morally or legally, for the imposition of compulsory eugenic sterilization on defective persons by twenty-five American states; see the author's "Sixty Years of Compulsory Eugenic Sterilization," Chicago-Kent Law Review, 43 (Fall, 1966), 123.

[9] But as Pope Paul told the United Nations on October 4, 1965, the best answer to the present population explosion is the "multiplying of bread," i.e., making the world more livable for its people rather than simply "diminishing the number of guests at the banquet of life." That birth limitation is not a panacea for population problems is the opinion of many demographers. However, it is one of several important factors. See T. Burch, "Population and Parenthood," The Commonweal, Vol. LXXX, No. 11, June 5, 1964, p. 328.

regulating procreation which are found blameworthy by the teaching authority of the Church."[10] In a footnote to the text the bishops cited the encyclical *Casti Connubii* and other Papal documents condemning contraceptive birth limitation. But except for a condemnation of abortion, the bishops refrained from commenting on specific means of birth limitation. In fact, they noted that Pope Paul VI had called for further investigation after which he "may pass judgment." "With the doctrine of the magisterium in this state, this holy Synod does not intend to propose immediately concrete solutions."[11] Some commentators have argued that this phrasing suggests that Catholics are now re-evaluating their opposition to contraception. However, it probably only indicates an openness to the question of what constitutes contraception and a desire to evaluate responsible parenthood in the light of contemporary reality. After he had received the studies of an international committee for the study of the problem, Pope Paul on October 29, 1966, reaffirmed the Church's opposition to contraception and described the magisterium as "not being in a state of doubt." Thus contraception and abortion are clearly unsatisfactory means of birth limitation for Catholics in the present state of the magisterium. There are some theologians who foresee a possibility of a change of position on contraception because papal teaching on the subject is based on a natural law analysis, and a philosophical natural law position is always open to examination based on the requirements of the human condition.[12] Other theologians disagree.[13]

Contraception

Contraception means the use of an artificial agent which acts as a barrier between husband and wife during intercourse so as to prevent the fertilization of the egg by the sperm. Contraception is an ancient method of birth limitation; some of the Fathers of the Church condemned the placing of sponges against the cervix, the pasting of crocodile or elephant waste in the vagina, and the practice of wrapping the penis in leaves. Modern physical devices operate in a way similar to

---

[10] Art. 51.

[11] Footnote 14 in the Latin text; footnote 173 in the Abbott-Gallagher English translation.

[12] See G. Baum, "Birth Control and the Council," *The Commonweal*, Vol. LXXXI, No. 9, Nov. 20, 1964, p. 280.

[13] See J. Ford and G. Kelly, *Contemporary Moral Theology*, Vol. II "Marriage Questions" (Westminster: Newman Press, 1963), pp. 272–273. Well-considered views on natural law and birth limitation are found in the books by Dupre and Grisez cited in the bibliography of Part III.

those primitive contraceptives; their principle is to cut off the sperm's access to the egg or to kill it. Thus, the diaphragm is fitted by a doctor to cover the cervical opening at the top of the vagina; the condom (prophylactic) is a glove-like sheath which covers the penis and prevents the sperm from even entering the vagina. In addition to these rather crude devices, man has developed chemical barriers. There are creams and jellies which, when placed in the vagina, kill the sperm. Aerosol vaginal foam accomplishes the same goal. Destructive chemicals of this kind are also available in tablet or suppository form. A newer, and extremely important, form of contraceptive is an interuterine device. Popularly called I.U.D., it is a metal or plastic coil which is placed in the uterus. Whether is is contraceptive or not has been debated since medical science has not determined exactly how it prevents pregnancy. It may be that the I.U.D. alters the environment in such a way as to kill the sperm; this would be contraceptive. It is also possible that I.U.D. allows conception but prevents the implantation of the zygote on the uterine wall; this would be abortion.[14]

These and other forms of contraceptive intercourse have been attacked by Catholic moralists on diverse grounds.[15] Some of the reasons given by moralists appear silly and superficial to married persons. A common argument is that contraception is immoral because it renders the marital act incapable of achieving the primary purpose of marriage, the procreation of children. That some who argue this way defend and even aggressively advocate the rhythm method of birth limitation is inexplicable.[16] The difficulty with this argument is that it requires one to accept the viewpoint that the begetting of children is the goal of marriage above and beyond any other good. Today, a growing number of theologians and married Catholics reject such a presupposition. Even those who accept the viewpoint that the primary purpose of marriage is the procreation of children refuse to equate procreation with physical reproduction.[17]

---

[14] See R. Ehrensing, "The I.U.D.," *National Catholic Reporter* (reprint), 1966. Ehrensing believes that I.U.D. is 98% effective as a contraceptive so that in 2% of the cases abortion is a possibility.

[15] Almost all Protestant theologians similarly attacked contraceptive intercourse at the turn of the century. The adoption of Resolution 15 allowing contraception for good reasons (but not "from motives of selfishness, luxury, or mere convenience") by the Anglican Bishops at the Lambeth Conference of 1930 was the turning point away from its earlier attitude by modern Protestantism.

[16] See, generally, the comments of L. Dupre in "Toward a Re-examination of the Catholic Position on Birth Control," *Cross-Currents* 14 (Winter, 1964), 66.

[17] See Chapter 6 of Part I.

Still another argument sometimes heard against contraception is that it is an artificial interference with the natural process of procreation. Of course, contraception is artificial, but no serious scholar today maintains that artificiality is itself the basis of immorality.[18] The argument is however, still frequently encountered at the pastoral level.

The contention that revelation rejects contraception is still advanced by some serious moralists. Usually they base their arguments on Gen 38:9–10 (the punishment of Onan after his interruption of intercourse to spill his seed) and 1 Cor 6:9–10 (Paul's condemnation of unnatural uses of sex). But this position is extremely difficult to maintain since all scripture scholars today agree that Onan was punished for his violation of the levirate law found in Dt 25:5–10, not for his interruption of intercourse. Paul does condemn unnatural uses of sex, but he lists these uses and contraception is not among them.[19]

A most reasonable philosophical argument against contraception, at least for one who accepts a Thomistic analysis of life, has been raised by Dr. Germain Grisez of Georgetown University. Grisez posits certain basic inclinations of human life. He believes that these inclinations can be demonstrated from anthropological and psychological data. When man achieves a knowledge of these inclinations, he can develop an understanding of the fundamental goods which human beings should strive to achieve in their lives and activities. Procreation of human life is one of these goods. Man does not always have to act to achieve these goods (every act of intercourse does not have to be directed to reproduction), but he must not act intentionally against them. "To act directly against any of the basic human goods is to spurn one aspect of the total possibility of human perfection, and it is freely to set the will at odds with its own principle of interest in the goods open to us."[20]

The most cogent objection to contraception is that it places marital intercourse in opposition to the nature of marital love. Physically and psychologically, sexual union is a striving toward an expression of the unity of one flesh. To place a physical barrier between husband and wife is to destroy the very expression which intercourse is meant to achieve. Some may think that this analysis places too much emphasis on the

---

[18] A leading philosophical opponent of contraception has written that "contraception is not wrong because it is artificial." See Grisez, cited in the bibliography, p. 166.

[19] Of course, one could not draw any conclusion about Paul's thinking on the subject from his failure to mention it.

[20] Grisez, *supra*, n. 18, p. 82.

symbolic value of sex. Yet, the symbolism of sexual intercourse and the means by which the feelings of total unity are communicated are fundamental to sex. Sexual union is like the loving communion of unity between Christ and the believer in the breaking and eating of the bread; a barrier between those in communion is unthinkable. To destroy the symbolism of unity, to cut husband and wife off from each other, is to strike at the fundamental experience of marital communion.

Coitus Interruptus

The oldest form of birth limitation is the withdrawal of the male penis before ejaculation of the sperm. This is so undesirable from every point of view that it has no serious proponent today. It makes female orgasm extremely unlikely and male orgasm much less satisfactory. It causes man and woman to draw apart at the very moment when the unified expression of love should be at its height. If practiced with any regularity, it will probably cause serious emotional problems in the marital relationship.[21]

Douching After Intercourse

The practice of washing the seminal fluid from the vagina after intercourse is ineffective as a means of preventing conception, although it is still used for this purpose by some people. Sometimes it is practiced by women whose puritanical education has convinced them that sex is dirty and male semen a cause of infection. Whatever the motive, the practice is inherently absurd, and constitutes a gross rejection of the love expression between husband and wife.[22]

The Anovulant Pill

It will be recalled that in Chapter 2 the hormone progesterone was described as inhibiting further ovulation during pregnancy and during the post-ovulatory stage of the female cycle. In 1955 researchers developed a compound from the root of a wild Mexican yam which

---

[21] See the comments of Allan Fromme in Sex and Marriage (New York: Barnes and Noble, 1965, tenth printing, paperback), p. 107; and F. X. Hornstein and A. Faller, (eds.) Sex-Love-Marriage (New York: Herder and Herder, 1964), pp. 57, 84, 197, 364.

[22] The postcoital douche and coitus interruptus are unanimously disapproved of by medical educators; see Tietze, Kohl, Best, and Eliot, "Teaching of Fertility Regulation in Medical Schools," Journal of the American Medical Association 196 (April 4, 1966), 20.

similarly operated to inhibit ovulation. This compound was named progestin. The use of progestin (or animal progesterone) in humans soon raised hopes that a noncontraceptive method of birth limitation could be developed for widespread usage. On September 12, 1958, Pope Pius XII took note of these developments and expectations and condemned the use of progestin as a means of birth limitation. He stated that the suppression of ovulation to prevent conception constituted sterilization.[23] This continued a line of thought developed by Pope Pius XI in *Casti Connubii:* that sterilization intended to cause infertility for purposes of preventing conception constituted an immoral mutilation of the human body.[24] Since Catholics do not consider bodily mutilation immoral when done to promote health or cure a pathological condition, Pius XII said that its use for therapeutic purposes would not be immoral.[25]

In the 1960's "the pill," as the compound came popularly to be called, gained common acceptance in the United States as a means of birth limitation. Several million married women were using it within a few years of its appearance on the market. Some Catholic moralists, writing in small-circulation professional journals or through privately circulated position papers, began to express the conviction that Pius' analysis had been made at a time when knowledge of the pill was too scanty. In 1963 Dr. John Rock, a Catholic who was professor of gynecology at Harvard University and a primary developer of the pill, attacked the sterilization-mutilation argument in a widely discussed book.[26] Late in the same year an internationally respected moral theologian, Louis Janssens, came to Rock's support.[27] Citing Rock's analysis of the effect of the pill, Janssens argued that there is no sterilization because nothing is mutilated; ova are not destroyed or lost, they are preserved in an immature state in the ovary. It was not long before another opinion, medical and theological, took issue with this analysis. Frank J. Ayd, a medical doctor on the faculty of theology at the Catholic University of America, contended that there was a sterilizing mutilation brought about by use of the pill. Specifically, he saw this in the sup-

---

[23] Address to the Seventh Hematological Congress, A.A.S., 50.

[24] A.A.S., 22 (1930).

[25] Supra, n. 23. Progestin is used to cure various menstrual disorders. It may also prove useful in preventing cancer of the cervix and breast.

[26] *The Time Has Come* (New York: A. Knopf, 1963).

[27] "Morale Conjugale et Progestogenes," *Ephemerides Theologicae Lovanienses,* Oct.-Dec., 1963, p. 39.

pression of ovulation and the alteration of the cervical mucus.[28]

On June 23, 1964, Pope Paul stated that in the present state of the analysis of the question in the Church there was not "sufficient reason to regard the norms stated by Pope Pius XII as being surpassed."[29] Implicit in this is the fact that the Pope considered the sterilization-mutilation analysis as still binding on the Church. But he also stated that further study might lead him to "modify" this position.[30] Such a modification would presumably result from a showing that the pill does not operate as a sterilizer or that it could be used simply to regulate the occurrence of ovulation.

A different line of argument over the anovulant pill as a means of birth limitation centers on its relation to the nature of marital love. Although some have held that the withdrawing of generative possibility by any positive means from intercourse is contrary to the nature of marital love because it denies the fullness of love expression which ought to be given,[31] moralists who oppose the pill have not resorted to this argument very extensively. On the other hand, W. Van der Marck, a Dutch theologian, agrees with Canon Janssens that reasonable family planning by use of the pill can be very much in accord with the Christian conception of marital love. Marital love, he believes, involves a willingness to enter into fruitful love and a reverence for the symbolic-actual love expressions of sexual intercourse.[32] He rejects contraception as contrary to the nature of marital love because it places a spatial barrier to the love expression of husband and wife, but does not see any similar objection to the anovulant pill.

A third question which has been asked about the morality of the pill relates to abortion. There is some evidence that the pill is not 100% effective in inhibiting ovulation in women who are using it correctly. Yet, if used correctly, it does prevent pregnancy.[33] Taking the pill does affect the uterine lining. Does this alteration render the wall unsuitable for the implantation of conceived life if ovulation should

[28] The Oral Contraceptives: Their Mode of Action (Washington: National Catholic Welfare Conference, 1964), pamphlet. See comment on Ayd's views in Ave Maria, Vol. 100, No. 16, Oct. 17, 1964, p. 27.
[29] A.A.S., 56.
[30] Ibid.
[31] S. Lestapis, Family Planning and Modern Problems (New York: Herder and Herder, 1961), p. 175.
[32] "Vruchtbaarheidsregeling: poping tot antwoord opeen nog open vraag," Tijdschrift Voor Theologie, Third Quarter, No. 4, 1963, p. 378.
[33] Supra, n. 28.

occur and the egg be fertilized? This is a possibility, but there are other explanations advanced as to why pregnancy does not follow. In the present state of our knowledge, one would have to conclude that abortion is one possible explanation of the effectiveness of the pill in a small number of cases.[34]

The side effects of the pill raise still another problem in judging its morality. Of course, any medical drug may have long-range, deleterious effects which can only be determined after a long period of usage. This fact of itself would hardly justify any opinion as to morality of the drug shortly after its introduction. At present, the United States Food and Drug Administration permits physicians to prescribe the pill; this is an indication that in the present state of our knowledge the pill is safe. However, some medical researchers have raised questions about the relationship of the pill to optic disorders, blood clotting, blockage of the arteries, some forms of cancer, and other undesirable effects. The F.D.A. has promised intensive research on these matters, and has required the pharmaceutical firms to list these possible dangers on the information sheets promoting the various brands. The F.D.A. hopes to provide a definite answer on the relationship of the pills to blood clotting by the early nineteen-seventies; it is estimated that research on the possibility that the pills create a predisposition to cancer will not be sufficiently complete to draw conclusions until the mid-eighties. One who wishes to judge the morality of the pill from the viewpoint of its safety can only look at the present state of the evidence and draw his own conclusions.

Chemical Compounds for the Regulation of Ovulation

Many moralists who oppose the use of the anovulant pill to regulate births on the basis of the sterilization argument have indicated that compound which merely regulates ovulation (and does not suppress it) would not be morally objectionable. The first drug claiming to regulate rather than suppress ovulation, duphaston, has proved unreliable. A number of individual doctors have claimed various techniques for the use of the anovulant pill merely to regulate ovulation; there is no general agreement as to how, or even that, this can be done. A recently developed drug, chlomiphene, has been shown effective as a means of regulating ovulation. Such an ovulant regulator, if it can be made

---

[34] Another explanation is that the alteration of the cervical mucus may adversely affect the sperm. This would be contraception.

available for widespread usage, would be invaluable to couples using the rhythm method of birth limitation.

Rhythm

It has long been known that women are fertile only at certain times, but it was not until Drs. Knaus and Ogino separately published their findings in 1930 that a means of birth limitation could be worked out on the basis of the female cycle. In his Encyclical Letter of December 31, 1930, (*Casti Connubii*) Pope Pius XI pointed out that Catholics had no moral objections to intercourse at a time when conception could not occur. Since sexual intercourse is an expression of marital love, the Pope could not have said otherwise. But could a couple morally confine their love-expression to periods of probable female infertility as a means of practicing birth limitation? If the couple had good reason to limit their family, this method seemed acceptable because it did not involve sterilization as did contraception. Pope Pius XII accepted this line of reasoning; he announced that he could see no moral objections to periodic continence as a means to limit conceptions for serious reasons of a medical, eugenic, economic, or social nature.[35]

Periodic continence, or rhythm, depends for its effectiveness on the ability reasonably to calculate the time of the wife's fertility (ovulation). This requires a fairly accurate understanding of the female cycle and a close attention to its progression. As has been mentioned in Chapter 11, there is presently no effective way to predict ovulation and only some very fallible methods for determining that ovulation has occurred.[36] A woman with an irregular cycle will have a prolonged period of "presumed fertility" which makes rhythm extremely difficult. Even the extremely regular woman (the great majority) will have a minimum "unsafe" period of ten days in each cycle after allowances are made for the lifespan of the sperm, etc. This situation has created doubt about the effectiveness and desirability of rhythm for many couples. However, many have spoken of rhythm as both effective and desirable.[37] Some studies indicate that a number of couples who find

[35] Address of October 29, 1951, A.A.S., 43.

[36] For a practical discussion of the means presently available for determining ovulation, see J. Marshall, *The Infertile Period* cited in the bibliography; A. Stecher, "The Practical Application of the Choice of Time for Coitus in Marriage," Chapter 13 of *Sex-Love-Marriage*, supra, n. 21, and W. Lynch, *A Marriage Manual for Catholics* (New York: Trident Press, 1964), pp. 190–213.

[37] See I. E. Georg, *The Truth About Rhythm*; D. Kanabay and H. Kanabay, *Sex, Fertility, and the Catholic*; T. S. Welton, *Rhythm Birth Control*, all cited in the

rhythm effective as a means of birth limitation are not enthusiastic about its effect on their total relationship.[38] If a method for accurately predicting or regulating ovulation is developed, reducing the "unsafe" period to two or three days, rhythm would probably become from every point of view a most desirable means of birth limitation.[39]

The Heart of the Moral Problem in Birth Limitation

Love and respect for life, and the means of transmitting it, are at the heart of the struggle among Catholics to work out a meaningful analysis of the problem of birth limitation. Although sometimes expressed in unfortunately heavy-handed language, it is the theme of statements by the magisterium on the question from Casti Connubii through the brief statement of the Second Vatican Council to the address of Pope Paul to the United Nations. Those who have demanded that the "Church give us an answer — tell us what to do" have failed to recognize that this is a "pilgrim Church . . . (who) dwells among the creatures who groan and travail in pain until now and await the revelation of the sons of God (Rom 8:19–22)."[40] As the people of God "see now in a mirror dimly" (1 Cor 13:12), they strive with great difficulty to understand God's plan for creation. What they do know is that the life God has given them, and the power of passing it on to others, is not a thing to be used lightly. Birth limitation, regardless of the method employed, does present a danger that our love and respect for life will be diminished.[41] Overcoming this danger, and working to make the world aware of the meaning and value of being alive in God's universe is the real challenge to the modern Christian.

---

bibliography. See also, S. de Lyon, "A Rhythm Clinic That Works," Sign, Vol. 43, No. 12, p. 13, July, 1964.

[38] In 1966, Dr. John Cavanagh, an advocate of rhythm, made a survey of 3,000 users of the method. The study showed that the strain and frustrations of the method can be great.

[39] On October 15, 1966, the Ford Foundation awarded a major grant to Dr. Jacques Ferin of the Catholic University of Louvain for the development of an accurate ovulatory indicator. This may indicate that science is close to such a development.

[40] Dogmatic Constitution on the Church, art. 48.

[41] See the thoughtful letter by Mrs. J. Walsh in The Liguorian, Vol. 54, No. 2, Feb., 1966, pp. 34–37.

CHAPTER 13

THE RESPONSIBILITIES OF
MARRIED LIFE

Togetherness in Role Expectation

It has been emphasized throughout that marriage is a state of communion by which two individuals seek an ever-deeper personal union with each other. The perfection of such unity is the one great task on which the success of all marital functions ultimately depend. Every activity in which husband and wife engage should contribute to this unity. The raising of children, economic planning, family religious life, and all the details of family life should be the result of love between husband and wife. Certainly, these activities should not be devisive of the husband-wife relationship, although this is actually what happens when either party begins to act unilaterally in respect to the details of family life. This is not to say that togetherness in family planning is the sum and substance of marital unity, but togetherness is a vital element of such unity.

There is a subtle danger in the attempt of husband and wife to achieve unity in the day-to-day tasks of meeting family responsibilities. In Chapter 3 of Part I much stress was placed on the fact that a man and woman complete themselves through unity with each other: the one person of the marriage consists of the complementary male and female. But this complementary union is achieved not by using one another as one would use a cosmetic to perfect physical appearance; rather, individual fulfillment results only to the extent that each one opens himself to the particular masculine or feminine person of the other. The spouse is not an object of functional convenience but a complex human being in whom one will find happiness only to the extent that he is loved as an individual human being. Marriage requires a most mature kind of love, the kind in which the loved one is dealt with for his own sake and not simply as an extension of the lover's own personality. This becomes crucial in role expectation. Before marriage, a man or woman tends to foresee the details of married life in terms of certain categories based on an idealized and subjective view of marriage. This conception frequently bears little relationship to the reality of married life. As the couple live and work together, they will evolve a realistic expectation of what daily roles each will accomplish. The danger is that a husband and wife might each continue to think and act in role expectation on the basis of their idealized, subjective conceptions. When this happens, they are merely using each other for their own convenience, rather than opening themselves to each other's personality. When married people habitually make decisions and plans simply in view of their own personalities, their marriage is in danger of becoming a mere union of two bachelors. Instead of seeking fulfillment in each other, they will be seeking it in themselves. Thus, facing such practical details of married life as economic planning and religious differences together becomes vital to the life of the two become one flesh. As such, these practical considerations have a place in the statement of a theology of marriage.

Facing Economic Reality

THE CHRISTIAN AND PROPERTY

The Christian believes that the right to property is not absolute, but is a right existing for and subordinated to the good of man. The use of material things should make man a better human being; in the case of the believer, it should aid the user to be a better participant in creation and redemption. In his Christlike use of material goods the Christian is helping to build the kingdom of God:

> Christians who take an active part in modern socioeconomic development and defend justice and charity should be convinced that they can make a great contribution to the prosperity of mankind and the peace of the world. Whether they do so as individuals or in association, let their example be a shining one. After acquiring whatever skills and experience are absolutely necessary, they should in faithfulness to Christ and His gospel observe the right order of values in their earthly activities. Thus their whole lives, both individual and social, will be permeated with the spirit of the beatitudes, notably with the spirit of poverty.
>
> Whoever in obedience to Christ seeks first the kingdom of God will as a consequence receive a stronger and purer love for helping all his brothers and for perfecting the work of justice under the inspiration of charity.[1]

For the married Christian the right of Christlike use of material goods is determined by the needs of family life. Because a family must be housed, clothed, fed, and educated, married people must be deeply involved in income production, economic planning, and utilization of property. "Spiritual" books which advise "detachment" from material goods are written for dream-world people. The married Christian must be deeply involved with material goods, not simply for the sake of possession, but in order that the family might continue to exist and grow. The remark of Ignace Lepp that moralists must stop speaking of property in the abstract is sound advice.[2] The following discussion of property problems in marriage will touch on only a few highlights, but as to these, the ideas presented will be specific.

Many Catholic commentators have discussed the right of property from the viewpoint of the individual and the state. But the familial right of property, a right having a firm basis in papal teaching, has been generally neglected. As the reader considers the diverse economic realities of contemporary married life, he should keep in mind the familial property rights described by Pope Leo XIII:

> The individual's right to property is complemented by the property rights existing in a man as the provider of the family. The right becomes greater with the growth of the human person in the family group. When a man has procreated a child, the natural order of things bespeaks an obligation to contribute to its growth through a provision of food and necessities. Beyond necessity, since the children carry his life, a father will naturally

---

[1] *Pastoral Constitution on the Church in the Modern World*, art. 72.
[2] *The Authentic Morality* (New York: Macmillan, 1965), p. 110.

wish to provide his family with that which will enable them to live decently so as to avoid as much as possible misery and uncertainty in life.[3]

Planning Family Economic Life

EARNING AN INCOME

Basic to a realistic approach to economic matters is the production of an income which will enable the family to accomplish the goals set out by Pope Leo. An analysis of income potential must be made even before marriage, and the inability to produce adequate income is a most reasonable grounds for postponing marriage. An honest evaluation of income status will have to be made frequently during marriage also. Before any decision about major property purchases, savings, obtaining credit, further education, or even the having of children is made, income must be evaluated. Many married couples are reluctant to discuss and analyze familial income. This reluctance can lead to a situation wherein each partner does his own private thinking about money until one day when they discover that their own private views of the family's economic status are quite different. Frequently, that day will be one of economic crisis, and it will be very difficult then to work together to overcome the misunderstanding which results from the fact of their economic bachelorhoods. Economic crises will occur in every marriage, but they can become overwhelming to the couple who have not learned to plan and evaluate their economic situation together from the very beginning of their marriage. Lack of joint economic planning will only aggravate a difficult situation, but the couple who have become one flesh with each other even in the economic sphere will find such a crisis an opportunity for further growth together.

Because both husband and wife usually earn an income in the first year or two of marriage, a couple can slip into an overly optimistic view of their income potential. But the dual income of a newly married couple can be a wonderful opportunity for planning. A good general rule would be that the couple who have a double income should live off the proceeds of one wage-earner's work and invest or save the second income. Many couples will use a stipulated percentage of the second income to make the vital purchases which accompany the founding of a new family, such as dishes, basic furniture, etc. Whatever a couple decide to do with the second income, the key to successful use of this

---

[3] Encyclical Letter Rerum Novarum, May 15, 1891, art. 13, A.S.S., 23.

opportunity is found in mutual planning based on a long-term view. If this planning is not present the couple will inevitably find that the second income has not contributed to the economic good of family. On the day that the second income ceases, the couple should be able to cite specific ways that it has been of benefit to them.

Income planning and evaluation should include a look into future potential. In the United States, the constant lengthening of the educational process, because of expanding requirements for economic survival, requires that the husband as the ultimate breadwinner secure the training he needs properly to provide family income. The cost of further education after marriage can be a tremendous burden both financially and in time, but it is a burden many young couples willingly bear in order to insure a more secure future. Student marriages have become an everyday phenomenon in American colleges and universities since the end of the Second World War, but they can generally succeed only where husband and wife are mature adults who have learned to plan and share the burdens together.

EXPENDITURES AND BUDGETING

Relating money spent to money earned is no easy task in a society which urges conspicuous consumption. From the moment that their engagement is announced a couple will be the object of innumerable promptings to buy, consume, discard, and buy again. In subtle and not so subtle ways every married couple is pressured toward believing that goods and services they do not need are essential. The techniques of advertising will attempt to persuade them that success in marriage requires X, Y, and Z products. To be a reasonable consumer in such circumstances requires great maturity. Basic to such maturity is planning of the quantity, quality, and cost of purchases in relation to income. Inevitably, this means budgeting of expenditures. Even if a couple doesn't budget every month, drawing a budget for several consecutive months in each year will give a couple some idea of the trouble spots in their expenditures.

Husband and wife should budget together at the beginning of the month. Teen-age children should be encouraged to participate. First, a review of the past month's expenditures as compared to the budgetary allowance for such items will give a couple a realistic budget. Everyday expenses should be very carefully reviewed at the end of each month, especially those for food, clothing, and automobile. These areas of expenditures can rapidly ruin the family economy if not controlled carefully. If, for example, a family is spending more than thirty percent of its income for food or more than ten percent of income for a non-income producing motor vehicle, important changes will have to be made in the use of such items or economic problems will almost certainly result. In drawing up the budget for the new month, the mistakes of the past must be eliminated. This is why the review of the past month is the first step in budgeting.

A sample budget is given below. It is not presented as an "ideal," for every couple will eventually evolve a budget form which is ideal for their needs and circumstances. Rather, this form is included as an example of the elements which will probably be found in most budgets. The student is urged to work out a copy of this budget, using a set of predetermined figures for incomes and needs provided by a friend, teacher, or his own experience.

Decisions to make expenditures should be based on the realities of economic status as revealed by the budgeting experience. Even educated people who otherwise order their lives carefully sometimes make their purchases carelessly and thereby create financial problems. Most people will shop carefully and calculate the real cost of large purchases, such as of a home or automobile. But a consistent making of small purchases on impulse rather than reason is the real cause of economic trouble in many families. The spending of money must always be deliberate and reasonable. The wife who shops from a predetermined list of needs will inevitably be more economical than the woman who attempts to plan a week's meals while she is confronted with the several thousand items displayed in the supermarket. A couple who obtain information on the qualities and prices of five or six different brands will inevitably make a more useful and economical purchase of a dishwasher than the couple who buy all their appliances from one store by habit.

The greatest problem facing those who are planning expenditures on credit is the determination of the true price they will have to pay. Many businesses which sell personal property make as much profit on the extension of credit to the consumer as they do on the sale of the item. Because he usually considers just the amount of the monthly payment, the consumer fails to calculate the total price he is paying and the effect which credit costs will have on his future budgeting. The

SAMPLE BUDGET FORM
Month of _____

Total income for month: $_____ (to be entered at be-
ginning of month)

Sources: Wages $_____
Interest $_____
Gifts $_____
Sales $_____
Loans $_____
Other $_____

Total Expenditures: $_____ (to be entered at the end
of month)

DETAILED EXPENDITURES:

EXPENDITURE:	ESTIMATE: (Enter at beginning of month)	ACTUAL EXPENSE: (Enter when expenditure made)
HOUSING: Rent: Mortgage Payment: Homeowner's Insurance: _____ :		
FOOD: Week of _____: Week of _____: Week of _____: Week of _____: Week of _____:		
CLOTHING: Parents: Children: Footwear:		

GROOMING:
  Barber Shop:
  Beauty Shop:
  Toiletries and
    Cosmetics:
  Laundry:
  Washing Expenses:

MEDICAL:
  Doctor's Visits:
  Medical Insurance:
  Pharmacy:
  _____:

EDUCATION:
  Tuition:
  Books:
  Supplies:
  _____:

HOUSEHOLD COSTS
  Furniture Purchases:
  Furniture Payments:
  Decorations:
  Repairs:
  Appliances:
  _____:
  _____:

AUTOMOBILE:
  Payments on Pur-
    chase Price:
  Insurance:
  Maintenance:
    Operating:
    Repairs:
  License Fees:
  _____:

INSURANCE:
  Life Insurance:
  Social Security:
  Retirement:

CONTRIBUTIONS:		
Church:		
Community:		
_____:		
TAXES:		
Income Tax		
Deductions:		
Real Property Taxes:		
Personal Property Taxes:		
Sales and Taxes:		
_____:		
MISCELLANEOUS:		
Savings:		
Hobbies:		
Smoking:		
Liquor and Beer:		
Banking Charges:		
Club and Organiza-		
tional Dues:		
Gifts:		
Babysitter:		
Family Recreation:		
Newspaper and Books:		
_____:		
_____:		
_____:		
TRANSPORTATION:		
Public Transportation:		
Parking Fees:		
_____:		
UTILITIES:		
Phone:		
Electric:		
Gas:		
Coal or Oil:		
_____:		
_____:		
_____:		

financing statement, signed by the consumer, never clearly reveals the true total price of the goods and the credit. The computation of interest and service charges can sometimes be difficult, but the careful couple will always consider these as part of their expenditure for the goods. For example, if a couple purchase a table for $240 and pay $40 down, they will realize that the total amount owed is not $200 but $200 plus interest and/or service charges. Service charges are the most common today, because labeling credit costs as such enables merchants to escape the usury laws governing interest. Reputable department stores will frequently levy a two percent service charge on the monthly balance due. Thus, the couple who purchased a table will owe $4.00 more than $200 before they even make the first payment. If the table is paid off in ten monthly installments of $20 each, it will take the couple one year to complete the purchase and they will have paid a total of $262, not $240, for the table. Smaller monthly payments spread out over a longer period will increase the cost considerably.

There are many less than reputable stores which are in business solely to drain an unreasonable profit from credit extensions. These merchants will frequently be able to add thirty to forty percent to the cost of the purchase by subtle credit manipulations. The law governing the extension of credit has traditionally favored the seller, but there has been a growing demand for legislation which would require the merchant to tell the consumer the true cost of credit. It should be apparent that a family must never commit itself to credit purchases until it understands the full financial implication of the commitment.

The use of general credit plans with particular merchants are a major encouragement to impulse buying. If a couple frequently make purchases under such a plan, the amount of interest (or "service charges") due each month will grow rapidly and often imperceptibly. Budget studies have shown that the cost of maintaining these credit plans are frequently one of the budgetary "leaks" discussed previously. Such a plan may be desirable for a family, but a monthly review should be made of its use. A couple should be particularly careful with the use of the popular "revolving credit" plans; these tend to encourage both impulse buying and increased expenditures for credit. Teen-age children should not be allowed to use the family credit plan except in rare cases; the parents must show their child how to make purchases on the basis of need and desirability, rather than on the availability of money or credit.

BORROWING MONEY

Every married couple will borrow money sometime. There are two questions a couple should ask themselves on these occasions; why do we want to borrow and from whom shall we borrow? As to the first question, they must weigh the purpose of the loan against the consequential financial burden. Borrowing for income implementation is generally undesirable since it will only decrease income in the future when the couple are repaying interest and principal. On the other hand, borrowing may be desirable and/or necessary in order to make a particular purchase.

Once it has been determined that a loan is desirable, the choice of a lender becomes critical. A good example is the largest loan a family will make — that which they will use as consideration for the purchase of a home. Every lender in such a situation will, of course, require that the family give a deed or mortgage on the home as security for his loan. Beyond this requirement, there are great differences in the kinds of terms which a family can get on a home-purchase loan. The best terms are usually obtainable from a credit union, which is a federally supervised savings-lending union open only to a specified class of persons. To those who are not members of a credit union, commercial banks and savings and loan associations are the best type of lenders. The terms available from these institutions will vary from time to time, depending on such factors as the degree of competition for mortgage business in the local market and the prevalent philosophy on the federal boards which regulate these institutions. The terms available will also vary according to the situation of the family. The greater the amount of savings which a couple have for a down payment, the better will be their bargaining power in negotiating a loan. Other lenders, such as finance companies, charge a much higher rate of interest than those mentioned above; their main mortgage business is with high-risk borrowers, a fact which might justify their high interest rates and service charge.

In obtaining a home-purchase loan, the couple should not overlook certain advantages which they may have because of some personal circumstances. Sometimes the husband may work for an employer who provides certain kinds of help to his employees in home purchasing; he may be a member of a labor union or professional association which will make loans available on better-than-market terms. He may be a member of a class for whom government legislation secures financial benefits in mortgage situations. If the home being purchased has a current mortgage, the purchaser might elect to take the property subject to the existing mortgage if he has sufficient funds to pay the difference between amount still due under it and the purchase price. This will be advantageous to the purchaser if the existing mortgage was negotiated for a lower rate of interest than is currently obtainable. In considering the purchase of a home, the couple may want to ask their attorney about the desirability of an open-end mortgage. This will enable the couple to borrow more money under the mortgage after they have paid off part of the purchase price loan. The attorney will be able to describe the usefulness of such a provision. It is particularly the young couple who are making their first home purchase who will probably not have a substantial down payment. This couple would be well advised to insist that the mortgage-loan agreement include their right to prepay. The right to accelerate their payments and thereby reduce the debt more rapidly, can help to cut considerably the total interest which will be paid on the loan as the family becomes more financially secure.

INSURANCE

The practice of hiring someone who will make the financial payments if a specified risk ripens into a determined event or condition is a very old one. Insuring against risks was at one time denounced by some moralists as gaming, but in the twentieth-century United States, it is a respectable, and in some cases necessary, form of gambling. Today, great numbers of Americans insure some aspect of the personal existence against risk: the risk of dying, the risk of negligently driving an automobile, the risk of a fire in their home. It is unquestionably true that some are insurance poor, but daily existence in a complex and competitive society usually demands that a family have certain kinds of insurance protection.

At least a small life insurance policy should cover the breadwinner in the early years of marriage; this protection can be expanded or adjusted to meet the means and needs of a growing family. Life insurance, of course, becomes increasingly more expensive as the insured person ages. If a policy has been in force for a period, the policyholder may find this is a valuable source for the borrowing of money.

Liability insurance is more than a convenience for the person who chooses to own an automobile. It is a matter of moral duty to carry such insurance, because if someone is injured through the negligence of the owner, the only practical way that the owner can fulfill his duty of just recompense of the victim is through insurance. Fire insurance on the residence is the oldest form of personal insurance; today, it is usually purchased as part of a "homeowner's" policy which protects against theft and liability to guests as well as against flood, storm, and fire. A couple ought to examine their homeowner's insurance every so often to determine if it is both up to date and that they are not paying for insurance protection which is unreasonable in view of their budget.

Annuity programs are growing in popularity today. An annuity is the opposite of a life insurance policy; in life insurance one is protecting the survivor against the risk of his death; in an annuity policy he is protecting himself against the possibility of living beyond a certain age. If the family is protected by a good retirement program, annuities are usually unnecessary, but many, independent, professional men find that an annuity program is the only practical form of old-age provision.

A couple should always be aware of their social security status. Although the law is being increasingly liberalized and expanded, some miss additional social security income after retirement because the wife did not work the requisite number of periods for eligibility. Looking ahead before retirement may enable the wife to become eligible without too much difficulty.

CHAPTER 14

GROWTH IN LOVE IN THE INTERFAITH MARRIAGE

Marriages between people of differing religious commitments are commonplace in the United States. About twenty-five percent of all nuptials celebrated in Catholic churches involve a Catholic and a noncommunicant.[1] Historically, marriages between persons of differing religions, races, or classes have usually encountered opposition from familial sources. But the marriage of a Christian with a non-Christian or even with a Christian of a different tradition has in recent centuries encountered an especially negative attitude on the part of Church leaders. This negative attitude actually began to grow in the first centuries of Church history. The Fathers of the Church who first propounded it were probably influenced by the Jewish prohibition of marriage with gentiles.[2] By 385, St. Ambrose

---

[1] Based on an analysis of statistics contained in the 1965 *Official Catholic Directory* (New York: P. J. Kenedy).

[2] See Dt 7:1–4.

of Milan could write: "there is hardly anything which is more dangerous than for a Christian to marry one who is a stranger to the faith."[3] In the fourth and fifth centuries, the Roman law forbade marriages between Christians and Jews mainly for political and economic reasons; the prohibition of marriages between Christians and infidels came to be part of the Canon Law of the Medieval Church. These prohibitions were frequently supported and maintained for pragmatic and nonreligious purposes, although the fear of a diminution of faith was also a factor. A negative attitude toward marriages between Christians of different traditions grew out of the bitterness of the Reformation. That this bitterness persisted for centuries is apparent from the following mid-twentieth-century statements:

> The Church strongly forbids marriages between two baptized persons if one is a communicant of an heretical sect and the other is a Catholic (Code of Canon Law, 1060).

> Marriage between Protestants and Roman Catholics is diametrically opposed to the eternal truths of God (Resolution of the Missouri Synod of the Lutheran Church, 1953).

> This convention earnestly warns members against contracting marriages with Roman Catholics (Resolution of the General Convention of the Protestant Episcopal Church, 1948).

> It is the duty of Christians to marry in the Lord. And, therefore, such as profess the true reformed religion should not marry with infidels, Papists, or other idolaters (Presbyterian Confession of Faith, Chap. XXIV, Sec. III).

These statements are still the official positions of the churches involved, but these policies have been made largely meaningless by the very numbers of interdenominational marriages and especially by the hard fact of contemporary ecumenism. As Christians search for ways to repair the scandalous disunity existing in the Body of Christ, they are increasingly coming to the realization that the one sacramental act presently jointly shared by the different churches is the interdenominational marriages between baptized persons. Although there appears to be a movement toward an eventual sharing of the Bread which is the Body of Lord, Christian marriage is the best present example of *communicatio in sacris*. It is appropriate, of course, that sacramental ecumenism be achieved through the sacraments of social unity, the Eucharist and marriage.

---

[3] *Letter to Vigilius.*

One sign of a changing attitude toward interdenominational marriages in the Roman Catholic Church is found in the decree *Matrimonii Sacramentum* of March 18, 1966.[4] The decree sought to remove some of the more blatant negativism which had characterized the attitude of Canon Law toward marriages involving mixed religion or disparity of cult. It seems to presage a more drastic overhaul of the canons on the subject in the major revision of Canon Law now going on. Among other things the decree removed the necessity for a written ante-nuptial contract by the non-Catholic which had been commonly used in the United States for several decades. It also made an effort to provide for situations in which the non-Catholic party feels that the oral, ante-nuptial promises[5] are an infringement of his conscience.

The decree further permitted the minister of the non-Catholic to address and exhort the couple at the end of the nuptials and to lead those present in prayer. Finally, the provision for excommunication of a Catholic who celebrates his marriage before a non-Catholic minister contained in Canon 2319 was abrogated.

Whatever the theological and legal status of interfaith marriages, whether Christian or not, there are bound to be day-to-day difficulties with differences in moral convictions, worship, and the education of children. Of course, this can be just as true in a marriage wherein there is unity of religion and cult. The fact that a spouse is a coreligionist does not guarantee that his fundamental moral values are identical to one's own. But such problems are more likely to arise in an interfaith marriage. Statistical studies reveal the depressing fact that both the divorce rate and lapse from religious practice are higher in interfaith marriages than in intrafaith marriages.[6] The difficulty with such statistics lies in determining to what degree the problems in an interfaith marriage arise from the religious differences or from the opposition such marriages incur from

---

[4] Issued by the Congregation for the Doctrine of the Faith with the express approval of Pope Paul VI.

[5] The promise made is a negative one: not to create any obstacles to the right of the Catholic party to profess his faith and educate the children to the beliefs of Catholicism. The positive obligations to do these things rests on the Catholic party alone.

[6] See "What You should Know About Mixed Marriage," *Ave Maria*, Vol. 84, No. 22 (Nov. 24, 1956), p. 8, and M. Leiffer, "Mixed Marriage and Church Loyalty," *The Christian Century*, Jan. 19, 1949, p. 78. The studies of three leading sociologists, Landis, Bell, and Weeks, show that a Catholic-Protestant marriage is three times as likely to end in divorce as an intra-denominational marriage. However, these studies were done before the impact of ecumenism began to be felt on thought about marriage.

parents, society, and the churches. This opposition unquestionably increases the burdens such a marriage must carry. Some studies have tended to show that religious differences are not of themselves as common a cause of divorce as drinking, adultery, temperament, and irresponsibility. The very volume of interfaith marriages in America demands that clergy, families, and society generally must undertake to develop more positive feelings toward them. This is not to say that interfaith marriages should be encouraged, but once they are contemplated and contracted, everyone concerned should work to promote whatever positive values can be achieved. The couple should be encouraged to develop a knowledge and honest respect for each other's beliefs; they may both discover that this knowledge and respect will better enable each to improve his or her own religious commitment. They should be encouraged to discover the moral values which they have in common and to make this the cornerstone of their life together. They should learn to develop a certain, common religious practice in prayer and Bible reading, in addition to the liturgical rituals which they practice separately in their churches. They should learn to discuss their differences openly and frankly, not allowing resentment about the other's religiously-based responses to a situation to silently build up. Those to whom young engaged or married couples naturally turn for advice, i.e., family, friends, and clergy, should urge the development of such qualities rather than simply presenting an attitude of disapproval.

One of the greatest problems in an interfaith marriage is the religious education of children. A Catholic parent believes that he is under an obligation arising from the divine positive law and ecclesiastical law (Canon 1060) to educate children in the teachings of Christ and the Church; under the natural law the education of the children is the obligation of both parents. This situation will almost inevitably cause serious problems of conscience for two dedicated parents of differing beliefs. Yet, a couple who have truly made their marriage a union of one flesh can be drawn even more closely together in their effort lovingly to reach a solution to this problem. Honest, mutual communion of minds and wills may not achieve a perfect solution, but it makes a better married couple and insures that the parents are working hard to make the children better persons and better sons of God.

The goal of any marriage is the building of a community of love, and this goal is obtainable even in spite of religious differences. If the husband and wife are Christians, even though of different denominations, the

kind of love they are striving to build in their sacramental union is
agapē; God's love given to both through Christ. In so doing, they are
at one in the very essence of Christianity (1 Cor 13), and their marriage
is a fulfillment of Christ's law of love.

A SELECT BIBLIOGRAPHY FOR PART III

An asterisk (*) indicates works available in paperback editions.

Babin, P., *Crisis of Faith: The Religious Psychology of Adolescence* (New
    York: Herder and Herder, 1963).
Barbeau, C., *The Head of the Family* (Chicago: Henry Regnery, 1961).
Bier, W. (ed.), *Personality and Sexual Problems* (New York: Fordham
    University Press, 1964).
Biezanek, A., *All Things New* (London: Peter Smith, 1965).
*Birmingham, W. (ed.), *What Modern Catholics Think About Birth Con-
    trol* (New York: Signet Books, 1964).
Bossard, J., *One Marriage, Two Faiths* (New York: Ronald Press, 1957).
Brooks, L. and E., *Adventuring in Adoption* (Chapel Hill: University of
    North Carolina Press, 1946).
Buck, P., *Children for Adoption* (New York: Random House, 1964).
Callahan, S., *The Illusion of Eve* (New York: Sheed and Ward, 1965).
Capon, R., *Bed and Board* (New York: Simon and Schuster, 1965).
Cavanagh, J., *The Popes, The Pill, and The People* (Milwaukee: The Bruce
    Publishing Company, 1965).
Clemens, A., *Design for Successful Marriage* (Englewood Cliffs, N. J.:
    Prentice Hall, 1964).
*Coudreau, F., *The Child and the Problem of Faith* (Glen Rock: Paulist
    Press, 1966).
*Dohen, D., *The Fascinating Female* (Glen Rock: Paulist Press, 1964) (origi-
    nally published by Sheed and Ward under title *Women in Wonderland,*
    1960).
Dreikurs, R., *The Challenge of Parenthood* (New York: Duell, Sloan and
    Pearce, 1958).
Dufoyer, L., *Maternity, A Baby Is Born* (New York: Alba House, 1964).
Dupre, L., *Contraception and Catholics: A New Appraisal* (Baltimore: Heli-
    con Press, 1964).
Firkel, E., *Woman in the Modern World* (Notre Dame: Fides, 1964).
Flanagan, G., *The First Nine Months of Life* (New York: Simon and
    Schuster, 1962).
*Frisbie, M., *Help Your Children Enjoy Books* (St. Meinrad: Abbey Press,
    1966).
*Fromm, E., *The Art of Loving* (New York: Harper and Row, 1956).
*Fromme, A., *Sex and Marriage* (New York: Barnes and Noble, 1965).
Fuller, E., *The Christian Idea of Education* (New Haven: Yale University
    Press, 1958).
*Gagern, F. von, *Difficulties in Married Life* (New York: Paulist Press, 1964).
——— *Marriage Partnership* (Westminster: Newman, 1966).

Gayeski, J. and D. and Burnite, A., *Search for Their Future* (retarded children) (Milwaukee: The Bruce Publishing Company, 1965).
*Geissler, E., *The Meaning of Parenthood*, 2 Vols. (Notre Dame: Fides, 1962).
Genne, W., *Husbands and Pregnancy* (New York: Association Press, 1956).
Gilbert, H., *Love in Marriage* (New York: Hawthorn Books, 1964).
Gordon, A., *Intermarriage* (Boston: Beacon Press, 1964).
Grisez, G., *Contraception and the Natural Law* (Milwaukee: The Bruce Publishing Company, 1965).
Guitton, J., *Feminine Fulfillment* (Chicago: Franciscan Herald Press, 1966).
Haughton, R., *Beginning Life in Christ* (Westminster: Newman Press, 1966).
*———— *The Holiness of Sex* (St. Meinrad: Abbey Press, 1966).
———— *What Is Marriage* (London: Ealing Abbey, 1966).
Hellyer, D., *Your Child and You* (New York: Dell, 1966).
Hettick, B., *Sex in Your Marriage* (St. Meinrad: Abbey Press, 1966).
Kanabay, D. and H., *Sex, Fertility and the Catholic* (New York: Alba House, 1966).
Knaus, H., *Human Procreation and Its Natural Regulation* (New York: Abolensky, 1964).
*Lepp, I., *The Psychology of Loving* (Baltimore: Helicon, 1964).
Lewis, E., *Children and Their Religion* (New York: Sheed and Ward, 1962).
Marshall, J., *The Infertile Period* (Baltimore: Helicon, 1963).
McGinley, P., *Sixpence In Her Shoe* (New York: Dell, 1965) .
Mihanovich, C.; Schnepp, G.; Thomas, J., *A Guide to Catholic Marriage* (Milwaukee: The Bruce Publishing Company, 1963) (rev. ed.).
Montagu, A., *Life Before Birth* (New York: New American Library, 1964).
Neuwien, R., *Catholic Schools in Action* (Notre Dame: University of Notre Dame Press, 1966).
Nevins, J., *Parent's Guide to the Catholic School* (New York: Benziger Bros., 1964).
*Newland, M., *We and Our Children* (New York: Image Books, 1961).
Noonan, J., *Contraception* (Cambridge: Harvard University Press, 1965).
Novak, M. (ed.), *The Experience of Marriage* (New York: Macmillan, 1964).
Oliver, B. and Daniel, E., *Woman: the Glory of Man* (Westminster: Newman Press, 1966).
*Oraison, M., *Love or Constraint? Some Psychological Aspects of Religious Education* (New York: Paulist Press, 1961).
Parker, E., *The Seven Ages of Woman* (Baltimore: Johns Hopkins University Press, 1960).
Popenoe, P., *Sex, Love and Marriage* (New York: Belmont, 1963).
*Pyle, L., *The Pill* (Baltimore: Helicon, 1964).
*Riker, C. and A., *Understanding Marriage* (Glen Rock: Paulist Press, 1963).
*———— *Understanding Parenthood* (Glen Rock: Paulist Press, 1964).
Roberts, T. et al., *Contraception and Holiness: The Catholic Predicament* (New York: Herder and Herder, 1964).
Rose Matthew, Sister, *Parent's Guide to Religious Education* (Milwaukee The Bruce Publishing Company, 1965).

Ryan, M. P., *Are Parochial Schools the Answer?* (Chicago: Holt, Rinehart and Winston, 1963).

Smith, E., *Readings in Adoption* (New York: Philosophical Library, 1963).

*Suenens, L., *Love and Control* (Westminster: Newman Press, 1962).

Terbovich, J., *The Faces of Love* (New York: Doubleday, 1966).

*Thomas, J., *Catholic Viewpoint on Marriage and the Family* (New York: Hanover House, 1958).

Trese, L., *Parent and Child* (New York: Sheed and Ward, 1962).

Trimbos, C. J., *Healthy Attitudes Toward Love and Sex* (New York: Kenedy, 1964).

*University of Notre Dame, *The Problem of Population* (University of Notre Dame Press):
Vol. I: *Moral and Theological Considerations,* 1964.
Vol. II: *Practical Catholic Applications,* 1964.
Vol. III: *Educational Considerations,* 1965.

*Watkin, A., *The Enemies of Love* (Glen Rock: Paulist Press, 1965).

*Weber, G.; Killgallon, J.; and O'Shaughnessy, M., *The Child and the Christian Mystery* (New York: Benziger Bros., 1966).

Welton, T. S., *Rhythm Birth Control* (New York: Grosset and Dunlop, 1959).

*Whalen, W., *Family Handbook of Dollars and Sense* (St. Meinrad: Abbey Press, 1966).

Zimmerman, C. and Cervantes, L., *Marriage and the Family* (Chicago: Henry Regnery, 1956).

The following periodicals frequently publish popular articles relevant to this part:

ACT, *Voice of the C.F.M.*
Family Digest
Liguorian
Marriage

The Children's Bureau of the U. S. Dept. of Health, Education and Welfare publishes an excellent set of pamphlets on pregnancy, child care, and education. A list of prices and titles can be obtained from the Superintendent of Documents, U. S. Govt. Printing Office, Washington, 25, D. C.

PART IV

THE HUMAN LAW OF MARRIAGE

INTRODUCTION TO PART IV

Law, Society, and Love

Because the "family is the first school of those social virtues which every society needs"[1] both the civil and ecclesiastical societies have developed a code which governs the marital institution. Through custom, legislation, or judicial determinations, human institutions have attempted to produce certain values in the marriages of their members. The Catholic who chooses to marry is bound by a double law of marriage because both the state and the Church have formulated rules which experience has shown helpful in achieving minimum marital goods in these societies. The non-lawyer tends to see in these rules a number of burdensome regulations, but he accepts them as the only protection against marital anarchy. The civil or canon lawyer sees these rules as a series of principles which grew out of practical human problems, and he knows that the marital law of any society is at best a necessary but imperfect way of

[1] *Declaration on Christian Education*, art. 3.

meeting the needs of both individuals and society. The danger implicit in any administration of marital law is that the rules can become for both layman and lawyer a goal rather than a means of achieving human values. The moralist Bernard Häring has suggested that all too frequently even the Church law on marriage has become so rigid and formal that the fundamental Christian value of charity has been lost sight of.[2] Law can never be perfect, but man must constantly re-evaluate it to determine if it still serves him or has come to dominate him. Today, both the law of domestic relations of the several states and the canon law of the Church are undergoing extensive examination, and important changes will undoubtedly be made in the future.

The Christian believes that the most fundamental of all values in human life is love (Mt 22:34–40; Gal 4:14–15). He believes that even the strictest observance of the law is nothing unless it produces love (1 Cor 13:3), but human law which is thoughtfully developed and virtuously administered can teach men basic values (Gal 3:24). Jesus reduces the whole law to love (Mt 7:12; Jn 13:34–35; Mt 22:34–40), but he also recognizes the need for legal regulations (Mt 5:17–19) if his work of love is to be accomplished. In reading the brief summary of legal regulations which follows, the reader will want to keep this question in mind: to what extent does law help the marital institution achieve its goals for the good of society and the development of love of the husband and wife. The good citizen or Christian will of course conduct his marital life at a plane far above the minimal requirements of the law, but he will also take an interest in making the law of marriage a better servant of Christ, society, and the individual man.

---

[2] "Rethinking the Sacrament of Matrimony," *The Catholic World*, Aug., 1963, p. 359.

CHAPTER 15

THE AMERICAN LAW OF
DOMESTIC RELATIONS

Historical Background

Family law in the United States is notable for its diversity. Responsibility for its development rests not with the national sovereign but with the fifty states. But in its fundamental conceptions of family life, American family law is marked by a certain consistency. Monogamy is uniformly enforced, free consent to the contract is required, a duty of support is always imposed at least on the husband, and the right to end the marital union is not personal to the parties but rests with the state. Much of this basic unity is due to the historical development of English family law by the ecclesiastical courts. In medieval England one of the few areas of legal activity to escape incorporation into the ever-widening power of the king's courts (common law and chancery) was family law. The medieval Church insisted on its right to determine problems relating to marriage. Every parish had a court composed of clerics and lay people in which marital disputes could be aired and hopefully settled with common sense, charity, and a bit of canon law. At the same time, ecclesiastical courts of diocesan rank were actually forming the canon law of marriage throughout Europe by deciding the difficult cases presented to them. This canon law was basically an updated version of the Roman law of marriage, although Christian theology and medieval philosophical conceptions of life unquestionably influenced it. As this law developed, the English ecclesiastical courts naturally applied it to pending cases. As the Church in England was gradually disestablished in the seventeenth, eighteenth, and nineteenth centuries, its courts became less influential. The power of hearing and determining marriage cases finally passed from church courts to the equity courts, but not until a fairly complete set of legal principles governing family law had developed. The equity courts did not have to develop a marriage law — they simply took over and enforced the law which had been forged in the ecclesiastical courts. This law was brought to the colonies and became the family law of the original states. With the growth of the United States this law in its basic forms was adopted by new states, although it was influenced by French law in the south central states and in some cases was overcome by Spanish law of marital property ("community property") in the southwestern states. When it met a territorial law which was completely foreign to its basic principles (as in the polygamy which for a time prevailed in the Territory of Utah), the Anglo-American family law prevailed. The discussion of specific rules which follows will point up some of the state-to-state differences, but the reader should not forget the rather surprising basic agreements which the family laws of the fifty states enjoy.

The Formation of the Contract

Some states recognize that men and women sometimes enter into a marriage agreement privately without a formal public ceremony or state authorization.[1] These "common law" marriages are not recognized in most states, however, and even where they are permitted, the marriage will not be recognized until a certain number of years has passed. To contract a marriage which has legal recognition from its beginning every

---

[1] Ala., Colo., D. C., Fla., Ga., Idaho, Iowa, Kans., Mont., Ohio, Okla., Pa., R.I., S.C., and Tex.

state requires the couple to secure a license before the nuptials take place. To be eligible for a license the parties must meet the minimum age requirements, normally twenty-one for the male and eighteen for the female, or eighteen for the male and sixteen for the female with parental consent.[2] The license will not be issued unless the couple also submit to a serological test.[3] Both parties must have sufficient mental capacity to consent knowingly and reasonably to the marriage; this will not normally be challenged unless a party has been adjudicated insane or feebleminded. When these requirements are met the couple is required to appear before the county clerk to secure the license. The clerk may be required to ask the couple certain questions under oath in order to ascertain eligibility to marry; he will always receive payment of the proper fee before issuing the license. This license must be presented to the witnessing priest before the nuptials, if the ceremony is to take place as scheduled.

Americans are generally free to marry any other person of the opposite sex. The principal limitations on this right are prohibitions of marriages between persons related by blood or marriage. These limitations vary widely from state to state; in case of doubt, the applicable local law must be determined. Some states also forbid marriages between persons of different races.

The nuptials usually may take place in any jurisdiction in which the bride and groom can qualify for a license. However, a few states have adopted the Uniform Marriage Evasion Act which voids the marriage of any domiciliary who marries in another state in order to escape some requirement of the local law.[4]

The Law of Support

The law governing familial support is enforced in two forms: quasi-criminal statutes which empower the state to punish a husband who willfully neglects to provide the necessities of life for his wife and minor children, and civil statutes which enable the wife and/or children to enforce the husband's support obligation through court action. Every state

---

[2] This is the age requirement in nineteen states. Ala., Colo., Conn., Ga., Hawaii, Idaho, Ky., La., Mass., Mich., Minn., Miss., Mo., Mont., Neb., N. H., N. Y., N. C., N. Dak., Ohio, Okla., Ore., Pa., S. C., S. Dak., Tenn., Tex., Utah, Va., W. Va., and Wyo. have slightly different requirements.

[3] D. C., Md., Minn., and S. C. do not require a blood test.

[4] Ill., Ind., and N. J.

imposes the duty of support on the husband; a few states pass the duty to the wife if the husband becomes incapacitated. The duty of support may be modified or eliminated as between husband and wife by a valid contract to that effect. When a child is emancipated (by reaching the age of twenty-one, entering the military, or marriage), the father is no longer legally bound to contribute to his support. As long as the father's duty of support continues in favor of the child, the father has a legal right to the child's earnings and service. What constitutes the necessities which the husband-father is obligated to provide is undefinable. It is determined from the circumstances of the family situation. Courts have held everything from minimal, nutritional needs to fur coats for the wife and college tuition for the children to be necessities.

Property Rights

Under the common law of England a married woman had no property rights. When she married, her property passed under the control of her husband. This may have been based on the husband's duty of support requiring him to have the concomitant right to control all family property. The husband's duty remains, but the American states have gradually erased woman's inability to own property after marriage. Today a woman is free to buy, use, and dispose of property independently of her husband. In a handful of states, however, all property owned by either spouse is community property and each has a one-half interest therein.[5]

On the death of a married person, the local law determines the interest which the surviving spouse has in the decedent's property. These rights, such as dower, homestead, spouse's award, forced share, etc., are frequently complex and an attorney must frequently be consulted in order to best protect the survivor's rights.

Annulment and Separation

The ecclesiastical courts which determined marriage cases in medieval England were sometimes asked to determine if a valid marriage had taken place according to Church teaching. A ruling by the court that what had apparently been a marriage was, in fact, a nullity was called an annulment. The power of annuling marriages passed into the equity courts and is today found in the domestic relations courts of all states. However,

---

[5] Community property states are Ariz., Calif., Idaho, La., Nev., N. Mex., Tex., and Wash.

the grounds for annulment vary from state to state. The most common grounds are lack of legal age, inability to consent to marriage because of mental incapacity or existing prior marriage, force, impotence, incest (i.e., marriage within the forbidden degrees of kindred), marriage in jest or mistaken identity. Because of the availability of divorce on grounds which are often easier to prove, annulments are not often sought in American courts.

A wife has the duty of residing with her husband and forming a marital community with him. Nevertheless, the majority of states permit a couple legally to live apart for a good reason. Sometimes, this "separation from bed and board" is a preliminary stage in a divorce action, but a separation decree can also be obtained independently of a divorce proceeding when marital incompatibility or the good of children requires it.

Decrees of separation or annulment are usually somewhat complex and extensive documents because the economic, social, and personal relationship of the man and woman are not always easily separated. The decree will usually incorporate reasonable contractual agreements between the parties, but sometimes the court will be forced to impose the terms.

Under the Canon Law a Roman Catholic may not seek a decree of annulment or separation from a civil court until the ecclesiastical court has given a decision in the matter.

Divorce

In every American state the courts have the power to dissolve the marital relationship if one of the parties is a resident. A divorce differs from an annulment or separation inasmuch as it is a complete voidance of an existing marriage. Unlike a separation, a decree of divorce confers a legal right to contract a new marriage. Grounds for divorce in many states include extreme cruelty, conviction for a felony, adultery, desertion, habitual drunkenness, violent temper, attempted murder of spouse, non-support, willful neglect, idiocy, insanity, impotence, and physical indignities. A few states permit divorce on the grounds of incest, epilepsy, fraud, leprosy, narcotics addiction, vagrancy, venereal disease, wife's refusal to move to a new home, or incompatibility.

The attitude of the Christian Churches toward divorce is quite important in view of New Testament teaching on the permanence of marriage discussed in Part I of this text. All Christian denominations recognize that a civil divorce may be necessary in certain cases. For example, a Roman Catholic whose marriage is declared null (nonexistent) by an ecclesiastical court will probably have to seek a civil divorce when a civil separation decree is either unobtainable or insufficient to solve economic or other problems. Except in situations of this kind, however, Catholics may not obtain civil divorces; in no case does Catholic theology recognize the right of the state to dissolve a valid, sacramental marriage.[6] On the other hand, many Protestant denominations recognize such a dissolving power in the state and permit their members to secure divorces when it reasonably appears to be for the good of the parties or the children.

The major theological problem with divorce is the question of remarriage (i.e., another marriage to a different person) after a decree of divorce. The Roman Catholic Church believes that such a practice is polygyny or polyandry and is contrary to the teaching of Jesus in Mt 19:3–9.[7] On the other hand, Christians of the Reformation tradition have developed varied laws on the subject.[8] The Canon Law of the Protestant Episcopal Church in the United States of America allows a divorced member to secure a judgment as to his marital status in the eyes of the Church from the bishop. If the bishop determines that the person is no longer married, and one year has passed from the date of the divorce decree, permission to remarry may be given (Canon 18). However, the Methodist Church forbids remarriage by a divorced person except in the case of an innocent person in a divorce action based on adultery or other conditions which constituted vicious mental or physical cruelty. In either of these cases, the Methodist holds that the evil action

---

[6] For a concise statement of the problems and duties of Catholic judges, attorneys, and parties involved in a divorce case see B. Siegle, Marriage Today, cited in the bibliography, pp. 228–231.

[7] The problem of porneia (uncleanness or unchastity) has never been settled. The Gospel of Matthew records Christ as saying divorce except for porneia is wrong (Mt 5:32 and 19:9). Is this an exception to the indissolubility? Catholic exegetes says it is not an exception, but support their conclusion on varied grounds. Protestant exegetes are split on whether porneia creates an exception. In this author's opinion the writer of Matthew's Gospel was verbalizing the apostolic decision that Greek converts must abstain from unclean things according to the Jewish law (Acts 15:29). A marriage prohibited under the Mosaic Law would have been no marriage in the early church: it was a question of validity rather than of an exception to the indissolubility teaching. However, the volumes written on the subject show that it is far from a settled exegetical problem. For a brief summary of the problem, see E. Schillebeeckx, Marriage, Human Reality and Saving Mystery, Vol. I, pp. 142–155 (New York: Sheed and Ward, 1965). See also note b to Mt 19:9 in the Jerusalem Bible (New York: Doubleday, 1966).

[8] For an analysis of the marriage law of the Protestant churches see J. Emerson, Divorce, the Church and Re-marriage, cited in the bibliography.

of the guilty party invalidated the marriage vow.[9] The United Lutheran Church in America recognizes the indissolubility of marriage. Through the resolutions of its conventions this Church does permit the remarriage of a divorced member. The reason for this practice is the Lutheran belief that marriage is a remedy for sin and that God in dealing with the sinner as he finds him provides remedies for his needs.[10] The United Presbyterian Church, U. S. A., recognizes remarriage after civil divorce only if the decree was obtained by the innocent party on grounds expressly stated in Scripture or implicit in the Gospel. The Presbyterian minister may witness the remarriage of a divorced member only if the latter shows sorrow for his past sin and promises this time to enter into a loving marriage for life.[11]

---

[9] *Discipline of the Methodist Church*, 1957, p. 130.

[10] Based on *Statements on Marriage and Family Life*, 1956 Convention of the United Lutheran Church in America.

[11] *Directory for Worship*, United Presbyterian Church, U.S.A., Sec. 10.

CHAPTER 16

THE CANON LAW ON MARRIAGE

Historical Background

The Canon Law of the Roman Catholic Church is an end product of many historical and theological developments. Even in the apostolic Church certain rules for the guidance of Christians in marital matters were developed. In fact, it would be possible to develop a simple code of ecclesiastical laws on marriage from the writings of Saint Paul. Paul gave his readers directions in such matters as the need for monogamy (1 Cor 7:2), abstinence from sexual relations (1 Cor 7:3–5), the duty not to separate or divorce (1 Cor 7:10–11), authority in the family (Eph 5:24), the duty of a father toward his virgin daughter (1 Cor 7:36–38), marriage to the unbeliever (1 Cor 7:12–16), prohibition of second marriages for bishops (1 Tim 3:2), and the proper treatment and duties of widows (1 Tim 5:3–16).

In the post-apostolic Church the development of legal rules governing Christian marriage largely resulted from the theological developments in the patristic age. For example, Saint Basil's recounting of Christian laws in his letter to Amphilochius reflects the development of Christian conceptions of life and sex up to his time. When Rome became officially Christian, Church Law began to merge with the Roman Law and to this day the influence of Roman legal principles runs through the Canon Law. The day-to-day experience of solving marriage problems in the ecclesiastical courts was yet another factor in the development of the Church Law, although legal precedent never became the central factor as it did in the development of the Anglo-American common law. The late Cardinal Stritch once stressed this element of experience in the development of Church marital law when he wrote that "through the centuries She [the Church], has had a great experience, and all of this experience she brings to her legislation."[1] The marriage practices of converted peoples also contributed to the formation of the Canons on marriage.[2]

New developments in theological thought and the press of contemporary needs require a constant updating of the law of the Church. The last major revision of the Code of Canon Law in 1918 witnessed some rather significant modifications of the marriage canons. The Decree Matrimonii Sacramentum[3] indicates that extensive revisions of the Catholic law on marriage can be expected in the future.

Canon Law on Pre-Nuptial Requirements

Betrothal contracts, although rare today,[4] are recognized by Church Law if they conform to the requirements of Canon 1017 that the agreement be in writing and signed. However, a valid betrothal contract does not create an enforceable obligation to marry since consent to the marriage contract must be freely given. It may, of course, create moral obligations according to its terms, especially if economic hardship results from

---

[1] From the Preface to Practical Manual for Marriage Cases by William J. Doheny (Milwaukee: The Bruce Publishing Company, 1938).

[2] Some of these influences are discussed in E. Schillebeeckx, Marriage, Human Reality and Saving Mystery, Vol. II (New York: Sheed and Ward), pp. 256–266, and in Zimmermann and Cervantes, Marriage and the Family (Chicago: Henry Regnery, 1956), pp. 43–46.

[3] March 18, 1966.

[4] Ante-nuptial agreements are common and desirable when the union is a second marriage for either or both parties. For example, when a widow with children marries it is advisable that she and her husband-to-be contractually plan the economic consequences of the marriage.

reliance on the contract by one party. It may also give an injured party the right to sue for damages suffered by the other's nonobservance.

Once a decision to marry has been made by a couple, one or both of whom are Catholic, the pastor of the bride is required to instruct the couple on the meaning of the sacrament (Canons 1018, 1033). The pastor is obliged to investigate and determine if the parties are free to marry (Canon 1019). In the United States this is normally done by a private questioning of each person under oath. If the parties have been baptized in other parishes, they must present their baptisimal certificates to the pastor who will witness their union.[5]

An announcement of the marriage must be made at Sunday Mass for three weeks preceding the nuptials (Canon 1022; this is commonly called announcing the banns). This practice dates from a decision made at the Fourth Lateran Council in 1215; its purpose is to enable any member of the community who knows of an impediment to the marriage to make it known to the pastor. Canon 1027 imposes such a duty on Catholics.

The Law on Impediments

An impediment is some obstacle to the formation or legality of a marriage contract. The law of the Church, like that of the state, forbids marriage to certain people or under certain conditions. In Canon Law there are two classes of impediments: impedient impediments make the union illegal but do not affect its validity; diriment impediments run to the nature of marriage and make an attempted union absolutely void.

The impedient impediments are:

1) A simple vow of virginity or a vow to receive holy orders or enter a religious community (Canon 1058).
2) Legal adoption of one party by the other (Canon 1059). This impediment exists only where the law of the state makes such a marriage illegal. No American state prohibits such a union.
3) Marriage between a Catholic and a baptized Christian of another denomination. This is the "mixed religion" situation discussed in Chapter 14 of Part III (Canon 1060).
4) Marriage between a Catholic and an apostate Catholic, a "public sinner," or an excommunicated Catholic (Canon 1066).

All of these impediments are dispensable under Canon Law.

---

[5] Decree of the Sacred Congregation of Sacraments, July 4, 1921, A.A.S., 13.

The diriment impediments prevent a marriage from coming into existence as long as they exist. Unlike the impedient impediments, which cause the marriage to be illegal, these impediments make a seeming marriage an absolute nullity. Most of the diriment impediments are dispensable, although the few that are thought to be based on the nature of marriage cannot be removed by any human authority. The dispensable diriment impediments are:

1) Age. A male under 16 years and a female under 14 may not marry (Canon 1067).
2) Disparity of Cult. A marriage between a Catholic and a non-baptized person is null and void unless a dispensation has been obtained (Canon 1052).
3) Ordination. The taking of major orders in a rite requiring a vow of celibacy as a condition of such ordination is an impediment to marriage (Canon 1072). (If this impediment is not dispensed, not only is the attempted marriage void but the priest is automatically excommunicated for trying to marry.)
4) Solemn Religious Profession. A person under a solemn religious vow of chastity is incapable of marriage (Canon 1073). (Excommunication is automatic for a religious who attempts marriage without a dispensation.)
5) Abduction. Kidnapping or forcibly detaining a person in order to make them marry results in the voiding of any marriage attempt taking place while the abduction lasts (Canon 1074).
6) Crime. The crimes which constitute impediments to marriage are: (a) adultery between the parties combined with a promise to marry while one of them is already married to a third party, and (b) the murder of one of the parties' prior spouses with the aid of the other party (Canon 1075).
7) Consanguinity. Blood relationship which is an impediment is of two kinds: (a) in the direct line to every degree, and (b) in the collateral line to blood relations to the third degree (Canon 1076).
8) Affinity. Relationship by marriage in the direct line or to the second degree in a collateral line would invalidate an attempted marriage (Canon 1077).
9) Public Propriety. If a man and woman have lived together as man and wife even though not married, or have publicly and notoriously

practiced concubinage, neither may validly marry any person who is in the direct blood line of the other to the second degree (Canon 1078).

10) Baptismal Sponsorship. A godparent (or minister of sacrament) may not marry the godchild (or person to whom he ministered the sacment) (Canon 1079). (The impediment of spiritual relationship arising from confirmation was abolished by the revised Code of 1918.)

11) Legal Adoption. When the civil law voids an attempted marriage between an adopted child and an adoptive parent, Canon Law also treats the union as a nullity (Canon 1080).[6]

The diriment impediments which cannot be dispensed are:

1) Tender Age. A person so young as to be incapable of consent cannot contract marriage (Canon 1067).

2) Impotency. If at the time of an attempted marriage either of the parties is incapable of consummating sexual union, no marital bond is formed (Canon 1068). Inability to achieve coitus renders a person incapable of promising total union.[7]

3) Existing Marriage. If either of the parties is already married to someone else, no attempt to form a union with each other can succeed (Canon 1069). (In the United States, a Catholic who attempts to marry in spite of an already existing union is automatically excommunicated. This rule dates from the Third Plenary Council of Baltimore.)

Consent and the Nuptial Ceremony

In order to form a marital union, the man and woman must freely consent to marriage (Canon 1081). This free consent is the very essence of the marital contract. In order to form adequate consent at least some understanding of what marriage is must be had by the parties (Canon 1082); however, a lack of knowledge of or even erroneous ideas about

---

[6] This should be distinguished from the impedient impediment of legal adoption discussed above. No American state voids a marriage between adoptive parent and adopted child; therefore, this impediment does not apply to American Catholics.

[7] This impediment exists under the law of domestic relations as well as under Canon Law. Mere sterility is not a bar to marriage under Canon Law but some commentators have expressed the opinion that a vasectomy, oophorectomy, or hysterectomy (all of which are sterilizing operations) create the impediment codified in Canon 1068. For a modern defense of this opinion, see Woywood and Smith, cited in the bibliography, p. 774. However, there does not appear to be a realistic basis for such an opinion since these forms of sterilization are now known not to affect capacity for sexual union.

the unity, indissolubility, or sacramentality of marriage doesn't prevent a valid consent (Canon 1084). Consent must be expressed by some outward sign, usually a word, between the parties (Canon 1088). This expression creates a presumption of consent, although the internal denial of consent by one of the parties will result in a void marriage (Canon 1086). If the consent is expressed through fear or force, it is invalid (Canon 1087); this is always a danger in a "shotgun" marriage which results from parental pressure to avoid exposure of a non-marital pregnancy. The expression of consent by proxy is permitted under certain conditions (Canon 1089).

Canon Law requires that marital consent ordinarily be expressed in the presence of the bishop or pastor, or of some cleric designated by the pastor (Canons 1094, 1095).[8] In danger of death or if it is foreseen that the priest will not be available for a month, Catholics may express their marital consent to each other without the presence of the clerical witness (Canon 1098).

Separation

Marriage entails the formation of a new community, the one flesh. The couple are therefore obliged to live a communal life (Canon 1128). But under certain circumstances such a communal life may be impossible. In such cases Canon Law recognizes the right of separation. Some of the grounds for separation which are expressly set out in the Code are:

1) Adultery. The innocent party may separate, unless he condones the conduct of the guilty party (Canon 1129).
2) Habitual criminality. If one party has developed criminal habits, and continues to exercise them, the other party may remove himself and the children from the criminal's household (Canon 1131).
3) Cruelty. Extreme cruelty by one party gives the other party the right to separate.

In these or other situations where a long or permanent separation is desirable, the facts must be presented to the proper diocesan tribunal. After the decree of separation has been issued, the parties may also have to seek a civil decree of separation or even divorce in order to insure reasonable, financial arrangements or to provide for the children. Tempo-

---

[8] This requirement was made legally binding by the Council of Trent, but since its decree (*Tametsi*, Denz. 1813) was not promulgated everywhere, not all Catholics were bound by the law. The decree *Ne Temere* of Aug. 7, 1907 (Denz. 3468) applied the requirement of a priestly witness to all Catholics.

rary separations for a good reason and with mutual consent (for example: if the husband freely joins the military or is sent on a protracted business assignment in a distant city) present no moral problem of themselves, and many canon lawyers are of the opinion that the Code recognizes them in the somewhat vague words of Canon 1128. Such separations can be a real burden to the union, however, and common sense would dictate that the couple should accept or plan such with great prudence and care.

Annulment

There are situations in which a couple who are seemingly married have not in fact formed a valid union.[9] A diriment impediment existing at the time of the nuptials, or a failure of consent, would result in a null and void marriage. The ecclesiastical courts have frequently been asked to review the evidence and determine if a marriage is valid. The petition attacking the validity of the marriage can be filed only by one of the parties (but not the one who has been the cause of the impediment) or by the official prosecutor of the court if the impediment is a public one.[10] No other person may attack the marriage by a court action, but anyone with knowledge of a null marriage may so inform the prosecutor. The validity of a marriage is always defended by a canon lawyer called the Defender of the Bond; one or both of the parties may also defend. Unlike the civil courts, there are no public trials in the ecclesiastical courts. The evidence is taken in deposition form; the judges rarely confront the witnesses or parties and arrive at a decision solely on the written evidence presented to them. Like the civil courts, these tribunals have provisions for the presentation of defenses by all parties who may be directly affected by the decision, for the calling of witnesses and for appeal.[11] A decision that a marriage is null and void is a determination

---

[9] There are two instances in which Catholics believe valid marriages are dissoluble. Because they are rare, detailed attention is not given to them in this text. Canon 1119 permits the dissolution of a sacramental non-consummated marriage by solemn religious profession or for a just cause. Under the law of the church only the Pope can grant such a dissolution. A non-Christian marriage is dissoluble if it qualifies under the Pauline Privilege (1 Cor 7:12–15). This permits the party converted to Christianity and baptized after the marriage to dissolve the union if the non-baptized spouse refuses to live in peace. Detailed discussions of the privilege will be found in these books cited in the bibliography: Cloran, pp. 262–265; Sheed, pp. 110–113; Siegle, pp. 211–222; and Woywood and Smith, pp. 873–883.

[10] *Instruction of the Sacred Congregation of the Sacraments,* Aug. 15, 1936, A.A.S., 28.

[11] The review is made by a court of appeals; appeals from this court can be taken to the Sacred Roman Rota. There is no appeal beyond the Rota unless the Pope chooses to act on the case.

based on the facts as they appear to the judges. The decision is not a declaration of divorce. If in fact there is a valid marriage, a decree of annulment will not void it.

A SELECT BIBLIOGRAPHY FOR PART IV

An asterisk (*) indicates works available in paperback editions.

Bouscaren, T. L.; Ellis, A., Canon Law, A Text and Commentary (Milwaukee: The Bruce Publishing Company, 1963) (rev. ed.).

Bouscaren, T. L., Canon Law Digest (Milwaukee: The Bruce Publishing Company, 1934 to date) (Four volumes plus annual supplements published so far).

Clad, Family Law (Philadelphia: American Law Institute, 1958).

Cloran, O., Previews and Practical Cases on Marriage (Milwaukee: The Bruce Publishing Company [multi-volume set]).

*Daly, C., Morals: Law and Life (Chicago: Scepter, 1966).

Emerson, J., Divorce, the Church, and Re-marriage (Philadelphia: Westminster, 1961).

Flood, P., The Dissolution of Marriage (London: Burns and Oates, 1962).

Goldstein, J., and Katz, J., The Family and the Law (New York: The Free Press, 1965).

Keezer, F. H., On the Law of Marriage and Divorce (Indianapolis: Bobbs-Merrill, 1946).

Kuchler, F., Law of Engagement and Marriage (Dobbs Ferry: Oceana, 1966).

Leavy, M., The Law of Adoption (Dobbs Ferry, Oceana, 1954).

McCauley, C., Whom God Hath Not Joined (New York: Sheed and Ward, 1961).

O'Mahony, P., Catholics and Divorce (London: T. Nelson, 1959).

Pospishil, Victor J., Divorce and Remarriage: Towards a New Catholic Teaching (New York: Herder and Herder, Inc., 1967).

Risk, J., Marriage-Contract and Sacrament, A Manual of Laws (Chicago: Callaghan and Company, 1957).

Roberts, R. P., Matrimonial Legislation in Latin-Oriental Canon Law (Westminster: Newman, 1961).

Sheed, F., Nullity of Marriage (New York: Sheed and Ward, 1959).

Siegle, B., Marriage Today: A Commentary on the Code of Canon Law (New York: Alba House, 1966).

St. John-Stevas, N., Life, Death and the Law (Bloomington: Indiana University Press, 1964).

——— The Sanctity of Life (New York: Holt, Rinehart and Winston, 1965).

Woywood, S. and Smith, C., A Practical Commentary on the Code of Canon Law (New York: J. Wagner, Inc., 1962).

Van Vliet, A. H. and Breed, C. G., Marriage and Canon Law (London: Burns and Oates, 1964).

*Zavin, T. and Pilpel, H., Your Marriage and the Law (New York: Rinehart, 1952).

A FINAL NOTE

Marriage and Eternity

What is the role of marriage in man's eternal destiny? When husband and wife have achieved final union with God, are they, who have struggled together, worked together, and loved together, to be separated? Jesus taught that "in the resurrection they neither marry nor are given in marriage" (Mt 22:30). The marital union as we know it will not exist.

But how do we know it? We see marriage now as the reflection of God's creative life and a participation in Christ's union with the Church. In eternity, man knows the Creator, not through images, but directly in all his Beauty. In eternity there is no Church, no sacrament. The symbols have become realities; the imperfect has been made perfect. Love remains as the perfecting bond. Can it be doubted that the creative love of God reflected in marriage, and the redeeming love of Christ symbolized in the sacrament, will also be perfected in eternal life? Pope Pius XII once said of marriage in eternity:

> Although the purpose it serves on earth no longer exists the marital bond has created such a union of love between husband and wife that they have become one with each other and with God. Their enduring love will exist through eternity.[1]

The first Pope told the early Christians the same thing when he described husband and wife as the "joint heirs of the grace of life" (1 Pet 3:7).

What will this enduring union of love be like in eternity? God only knows. But the Christian knows that it will be a personal union of great joy because he who is Love cannot but give such to those whose vocation in life has been to love him in each other.

What no eye has seen, nor ear heard
Nor the heart of man conceived
What God has prepared for those who love him (1 Cor 2:9).

---

[1] Talk of April 29, 1942.

SUBJECT INDEX

INDEX OF NAMES

on familiar property, 119 f; on marriage and the Incarnation, 25 n; on the origin of marriage, 13; on pre-Christian sacramental character of marriage, 15 f

Lepp, Ignace, on morals & property, 119

Martin of Tours, anti-sexual ideas of, 31
Mirgeler, Arthur, on adoption, 95 n

Newman, Cardinal, on growth, 86
Nietzsche, Friedrich, contempt for virtuous man, 4; definition of marriage, 17
Novak, Michael, on sexual love, 86
Noonan, John T., on birth control, 104 f

Origin, and the "spiritual" nature of man, 13 n

Paul, St., on adoption, 95 f; on Christian communion, 74; directions on marriage, 148; on indissolubility, 21; on liturgy, 27; and the sacraments, 24 f; on the union of husband & wife, 26; and unnatural uses of sex, 110
Paul VI, Pope, on anovulant pill, 113; on importance of the birth control problem, 9; on interdenominational marriages, 132; on means of birth limitation, 108

Pius XI, Pope, on the institution of marriage, 12 n; on the origin of marriage, 13; on parents as primary educators, 98; and rhythm, 115; on sterilization, 112
Pius XII, Pope, on anovulant pill, 112 n; on marriage and eternity, 156; on reason for indissolubility, 21; and rhythm, 115

Rahner, Karl, on nature, 11 n
Rock, John, defends use of anovulant pill, 112

Scheeben, Matthias, on union of husband & wife in Christ, 26 f
Sirius, Pope, on liturgical betrothal, 64

Tertullian, on Christ's presence in marriage, 26; and sex, 31
Tillman, Fritz, on prudish ideas, 49

Van der Marck, W., defends use of anovulant pill, 113
Vincent of Lerins, on sin in sexual intercourse, 32
Von Rad, Gerhard, and Gen. 1:27, 14